PREFACE.

THE Mission of the West Indian Church to Western
Africa was inaugurated in the year 1851, although
its actual work was not commenced on the banks of
the Rio Pongo before the summer of 1855. After
less than a two years' residence in that country, its
first missionary, the Rev. Hamble James Leacock,
was cut off by death just as the arduous work he had
undertaken was giving the promise of great success.
Early in 1857 the first secretary to the English
Committee, Dr. Henry Caswall, published the life of
Leacock under the title of the "Martyr of the
Pongas." This book was in no sense a history of the
Mission, which was only then in its infancy and had
but a year's history to record. Since then, nearly
half a century has passed away, and no attempt has
been made to give a consecutive story of the Mission
which has continued its efforts to the present time.
Amid untold difficulties and discouragements, a little
band of missionaries, catechists, and schoolmasters
have struggled on and persevered ; and one by one,
as they have rested from their labours, their places
have been filled. Indeed, the combined records of
the extension of Christianity could scarcely afford a
nobler example of how the Gospel may, with the

Divine help, be effectually propagated. Of the
courage, the self-devotion, and the zeal which have
characterized the efforts of these few labourers, it is
not the special object of these pages to speak; but
they are sent forth to tell their own tale in the hope
that the blessing of God may rest upon them, and
that they may win the favourable consideration of
Christian people.

The sources of information have been Dr. Caswall's
" Martyr of the Pongas," and Bishop Parry's " History
of the Early Days of the Mission," published many
years ago in the *Mission Field.* In addition to these,
the present author has made full use of the " Story
of the Mission," * continued the story to the present
time, and given such other information as his office
of Secretary for the last seventeen years has naturally
brought him. The original intention to give a faithful record of all events has not, however, been carried
out, as just half of the manuscript has had to be set
aside in order to bring the book down to its present
proportions. This will account for the omission of
a large number of incidents and the somewhat
journalistic form of the closing chapters. Many
thanks are due to the Rev. Professor Caldecott and
the Rev. Canon Bindley for their kind assistance and
revision of the manuscript.

March, 1900.

* Compiled in "the eighties" by the Rev. J. R. Izat, Vicar of
Streatley and Assistant-Secretary of the Mission.

COMMENDATORY NOTE

BY THE PRIMATE OF THE WEST INDIES.

———•◦•———

THE readers of this book will find it to be an interesting story of the West Indian Mission to West Africa, often called the Rio Pongo Mission. The writer, as Secretary of the Committee in England, has given much time and labour to promoting this enterprise, and is well acquainted with the facts. A connected account of the beginnings and later progress of the Mission was much needed, and I hope the story herein told will encourage its old friends to continue their efforts, and will help to raise up new friends both in England and in the West Indies.

This Mission is only a small one, but it is the embodiment of a great and fruitful idea, and has already done much to quicken, among the people of the West Indies, a desire to make known the Gospel of Christ in that land from which the forefathers of many of them came.

I commend the book to the attention of those who desire to become acquainted with genuine efforts made for the extension of the Kingdom of Christ, and the Mission itself to their prayers and sympathetic help.

E. JAMAICA,

Primate of the West Indies.

LONDON, *July* 20, 1899.

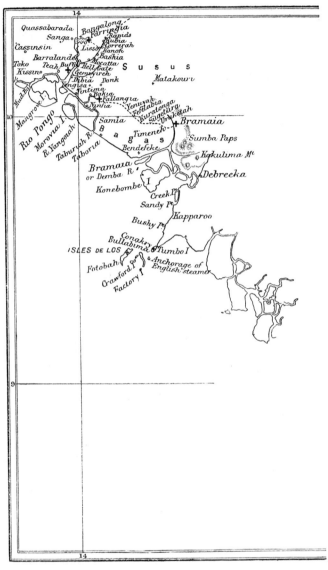

14

Quassabarada
Sanga
Cassinsin
Barralande
Toko   Teak Buff
Kissine
Tibia   Donk
Jintima
Bakia
Ninha   Fallangra
Samia   Yenuyah
Fetlabia
Kuralonga
Sugetira
Urukalah
Bangalong
Farringia
Rapids
Aubia
Correrah
Hanoh
Bashia
Mocatta
Hell Gate
Gemoyireh
Lissor
S u s u s
Matakouru
Bramaia
Timeneh
Bendefeke
Sumba Paps
Kakulima Mt
Bramaia
or Demba R
Debreeka
Konebombe
Creek Pt
Sandy Pt
Bushy Pt
Kapparoo
Conakry
Bullabima   Tumbo I
ISLES DE LOS
Fotobah
Crawford I
Factory
Anchorage of
English steamer
Rio Pongo
Morovia I
R.Yangoah
Taburjah R.
Taboria
Mangrove I.
Mud Bt
B a g a s
10

9

14

NOTE.—Owing to the printing of the Map on two pages, the coast-line

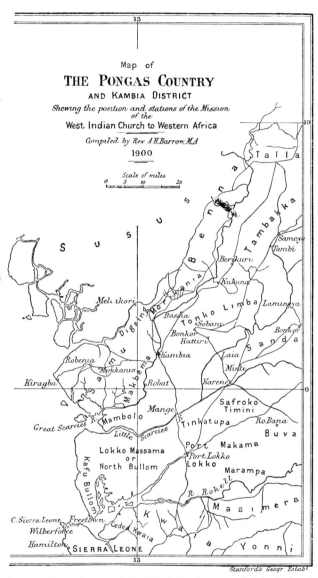

between Sierra Leone and the Isles de Los becomes slightly displaced.

FIFTY YEARS IN WESTERN AFRICA.

— ⚫ —

CHAPTER I.

Introductory—Idea and purpose of the mission—Reflections of Principal Rawle—Codrington College—Practical outcome—Pongas country—The Rio Pongo—Abortive effort by C.M.S.—Climate—Fevers—Tornado—Scenery—The White Ant—The Susu tribes—Form of government—Customs—Art of healing—Religious ideas—Mohammadanism—Contrasted with Christianity, etc.

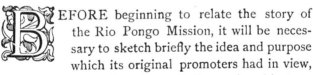EFORE beginning to relate the story of the Rio Pongo Mission, it will be necessary to sketch briefly the idea and purpose which its original promoters had in view, to offer some explanations of the main object to which its inception was due, and also to give a few particulars of the Pongas country and the Susu tribes amongst whom the missionaries labour. First of all, then, it must be clearly understood that this Mission was the outcome of a noble effort of missionary zeal on the part of the West Indian Church. To that Church it owes its birth, and from that Church it has ever derived its main support. There were many just and good reasons for this, as well as for the

choice of that particular part of Africa which was decided on as its field of work.

The West Indian Church has within her fold many whose ancestors were born, lived, and died on the Rio Pongo. These Christians could not forget their fatherland, and naturally the thought occurred to them, as well as to their teachers, the clergy who had brought them to Christ, "Can nothing be done by us to carry the message of the Gospel to those of our own flesh and blood in far-off Africa?" Africa's children felt they owed a debt to her, but there were others who were equally indebted, viz. the Christian Europeans in, and connected with the West Indies. It was a claim of justice as well as charity, that restitution be made to those who had been wronged in the past. To undo the past was impossible, but nevertheless it was possible to do something to root out the remains of that slavery which, even now, after so many years of Christian influence, continues a blot upon the progress of African civilization. And this claim of Africa was not confined to the West Indian colonies, but addressed itself to all British subjects ; for the old slave-trade, which brought the negro of Western Africa to the West Indies, did not originate in the efforts or wishes of the colonists, but against their wishes and remonstrances—in the policy of the mother country. Thoughts like these led to the formation of an association in the West Indies for the furtherance of the Gospel in Western Africa.

The idea may have occurred to more than one West Indian Churchman : certainly Bishop Parry of Barbados had conceived it, when, in answer to an invitation from the S.P.G. inviting co-operation in the celebration of the Society's third jubilee he wrote as follows, April 14, 1851 :— *

"The chief commemoration of the jubilee which I propose in my own diocese, and venture to suggest also to the other West Indian bishops, is to commence an African Mission, if only in answer to our prayers and efforts the great Lord of the Harvest be pleased to send forth the labourers, disposing also the members of the West Indian Church to unite in the work, and others in England to assist it. I am fully aware how far from attractive is the missionary field which the Western Coasts of Africa present; how trying the climate; how degraded the people; and how slow, probably, the progress will be in anything lovely and of good report. Still it is a work which ought to be done, which has, indeed, in more than one place been already commenced, and in which the West Indian Church should certainly take a part. If the Society's jubilee should find us at length engaged in it, surely it would be a suitable commemoration of the Society's benefits, to be thus, after a century and a half given to America and Asia, thinking also of Africa." †

* It is of interest to note that after the lapse of another fifty years, and whilst celebrating its Bicentenary, the Society is helping the Pongas Mission, in its first jubilee, to build churches in Western Africa (see note p. 61).

† "S.P.G. Digest," 1898. The succeeding paragraphs in the Digest (p. 264) fully explain the unbroken connection which has existed between the parent society and the Pongas Mission :—

"At the Barbados Church Society's meeting (S.P.G.), June 16, 1851 —which also happened to be the jubilee day of the Society—it was determined to make the African Mission not a mere branch of the Church Society's operations, but the object of a distinct organization,

This was the living idea which afterwards took a practical shape in the mind of Mr. Rawle, Principal of Codrington College, Barbados (afterwards the first Bishop of Trinidad). This singularly gifted man, after a remarkable record at Cambridge, was holding a Trinity College living, when he decided to offer himself for missionary service. The S.P.G. hailed his offer as most timely, for Codrington College at that time was without a Principal. The foundation of this noble institution was due to the far-sighted conception of a West Indian layman in the reign of Queen Anne, and its purpose, the raising up of faithful clergy and instructed laity in the churches of the West Indies, was one which was wholly congenial to the talents and sympathies of Mr. Rawle. When he was settled at the college he found that its windows looked direct across the Atlantic to West Africa. Surrounded as he was by liberated Africans, for whose spiritual and moral benefit assiduous efforts were being made by Christians of all denominations at home, he could not but send his thoughts far out to their ancestral tribes. And thus the idea came to birth in a master-mind.

In 1850, after consultation with Bishop Parry, he prepared a speech for the annual S.P.G. meeting at Bridgetown, Barbados, in which he pressed upon a

to be called—in the hope of that general co-operation already contemplated—'The West Indian Church Association for the furtherance of the Gospel in Western Africa, in connection with the S.P.G., as Trustees of Codrington College.'

"Towards the Mission the Society appropriated, in February, 1851, an allowance from the Codrington Trust Property for the Education of Missionaries ; and (in 1852) £1000 was voted from the Jubilee Fund as an endowment, a like sum being at the same time granted in aid of the endowment of a bishopric at Sierra Leone."

crowded audience the immediate steps which should be taken to inaugurate such a mission.

With burning eloquence he depicted the wrongs which, up to the beginning of the present century, had been inflicted by the slave trade on Western Africa. He urged the claims of that dark land, upon the sympathies of Christian hearts, on the ground that it had furnished nine-tenths of the population of the Caribbean Islands, on whose labour alone they were dependent, at that time, for the cultivation of their fruitful soils. He maintained that Codrington College should be utilized to prepare young men of African descent for the work of Evangelists, who were willing to offer themselves, and who showed an aptitude for the high calling. "We look from our windows," he said, "straight towards that dark land : there lies only the wide Atlantic between our college and Western Africa, and she seems to stretch out her hands to us to-day, and say, ' Come over and help us ! "

The idea was at once taken up, and it was not long before the western portion of the Principal's own lodge at Codrington was prepared for the reception of half a dozen students of African blood. A fund for the maintenance of these, and for the endowment of the Mission, was then set on foot, and was readily supplemented by contributions from England, given by friends of the Principal, and from his old parishioners at Cheadle. The college staff followed the example of their Head, and took their share in the tuition of the students; and in 1855 John Duport, a coloured man who had received his education at one of the primary schools in St. Kitts, had been sufficiently prepared for Holy Orders to accompany to Africa the Rev. H. T. Leacock. the pioneer of the Mission.

It will now be appropriate to give some little information respecting the Pongas country and its inhabitants. It will suffice, for the purpose, to say that the country is situated on the coast of Western Africa, about 100 miles to the north of Sierra Leone, whilst the Mission itself is bounded on the north by the Rio Nunez, and on the south by the River Dubrika. Eastwards and landwards it has no boundary, let us hope. It includes also the Isles de Los : some small but very beautiful islands opposite the mouth of the River Dubrika, and belonging, happily, to Great Britain. They are a group of seven islands to which the Portuguese gave the name of Yolas de los Idolos (Islands of Idols). Three are inhabited, the other four being nothing more than a shapeless mass of volcanic *débris*. They are well situated, as regards the mainland, opposite the mouths of the Dubrika and Dembia rivers, which are easy of access, and are the centre of a considerable trade. As the crow flies they are 35 miles distant from Bramaia, the easiest route being up the Dubrika and Bramaia rivers. Colonel Chamberlayne, the acting Governor of Sierra Leone, writing in February, 1865, says of them : " All persons whom I have consulted agree in considering the isles an excellent position for a Mission. The salubrity of the isles would enable the missionaries to enjoy some amount of health, and their proximity to Sierra Leone would enable them to obtain supplies, advice, and change of air without trouble."

Situated nearly midway between the Rio Pongo and Sierra Leone, or about 50 miles from Fallangia, they are hilly, well watered, and wooded, and are far enough from the coast to be entirely free from the poisonous malaria of the low, marshy ground of the river banks.   They lie, too, in the regular highway of the coast traffic of Africa.

The name "Rio Pongo" (or the mud river) was given to it, most probably in the fifteenth century, by the Portuguese, who visited this district as well as Sierra Leone (then called Tegaria) in search of slaves to supply the labour-market, of St. Domingo.   We read that Cardinal Ximenes, the celebrated Biblical scholar who was Archbishop of Toledo in 1507, did all in his power to discourage the trade.   The Roman Catholic clergy, however, upheld it, saying that they found it easier to convert the natives to Christianity when they where removed from the influence of their superstitions.

In early days they made many converts, and it is interesting to us to learn that their first were baptized in the waters of the Rio Pongo.   Of the later history of their Mission, and its results, we know very little.

The river itself consists of an estuary of several streams, which meet at a short distance from the sea, and empty their waters through a muddy channel, into the Atlantic.   Across the mouth of this estuary, which is nearly three miles wide, there are several islands, the largest of which is called Mangrove Island.   There are seven entrances in all, each one being more or less blocked by a bar. The best of these entrances is called the Sandbar Passage, on the south side of Mangrove Island. At a distance of about four miles from this passage, on the southern bank of the stream, the Little Pongo enters the river from the south-east. Following it up about five miles above its junction with the Great Pongo, we reach Tintima where the first missionary landed; and twelve miles higher up the same stream is Fallangia, where the first Station was planted. Returning to the point where we left the Great Pongo, and proceeding up it, we pass Boffa on the north bank, distant some thirteen miles from the sandbar. Here the French commandant of the river lives, and there is also a Roman Catholic mission-station. Two miles farther on the same side of the river is Domingia, for many years one of the chief Stations of the Mission. One of the old Reports calls Fallangia the Canterbury, and Domingia the London of the Mission. A few miles above Domingia we pass an uninhabited, magnificent volcanic island, known as Devil's Island, which forms the channel called by the ill-omened name of Hell's Gate, in which there is at times a dangerous whirlpool, where many slave-ships have been lost. Here two streams meet and form the Rio Pongo proper. One comes from the north and is called the Bangalong, at the head of which, and at a distance of eight miles from Devil's Island, stands Farringia on the side of a kind of wide lagoon. The other stream, the Fattalah, comes from the north-east, taking its rise in the Fullah country at least 150 miles off. The Fattalah is an exceedingly beautiful river, becoming more lovely the higher you ascend. About thirity miles from the sea navigation is stopped by rapids, but above the rapids are several falls, beyond which it is possible to travel on the river by boat for a month.

Early in the year 1798 two medical missionaries, Henry Brunton and Peter Greig, were sent by the Scotch Presbyterian church to "*the land of the Susus.*" They met with but little success. Greig was cruelly murdered at Kubia, on the Fattalah River, by a party of Fullahs, instigated by a desire of plunder, and their labours were not followed up.

In the year 1807 the attention of the Church Missionary Society was directed, in the first instance, to the Susus because their language was understood by several other tribes, both on the coast and in the interior ; and because, of all the numerous languages of Western Africa, it was the first reduced to writing, several books of religious instruction having been printed in Susu at an early period. Accordingly, after some preliminary explorations, the first Mission station amongst the Susus was opened, in 1808, at Bashia, on the Fattalah River, and a few years later, Kanofi, on the same river was occupied.

In 1815 a missionary settlement called Gambier (after Lord Gambier, then president of the C.M.S.) was opened among the Bagas, at Kapparu, about seventy miles north of Freetown, at the mouth of the Dubrika River. These pioneering efforts were carried on under the most discouraging circumstances, and were attended with most serious loss of life. In eleven years fifteen missionaries had gone forth, of

whom seven were early victims to the climate. In
1817 the slave-trade revived, and, at the instigation
of the slave-dealers, the Mission buildings were
destroyed by fire. On all sides the opposition
became so formidable that the missionaries were
compelled to withdraw from the settlements they had
formed, and take refuge in Sierra Leone. Then
followed a time when darkness spread over the land
like a cloud; but still God was not without His
witness—the prayers of one faithful penitent were
rising up day by day to the throne of grace until, in
His own good time, the Light of Truth once more
returned.

The climate is an obstacle to the Mission, but
there are two qualifying considerations; the one, that
an improved system of medical treatment in the
acclimating fever has been at least partially successful
on the coast during past years; the other, that West
Indians, and especially coloured persons, though not
perhaps *proof* against the African climate, would
suffer less from it than Europeans. The heat, which
is so fearfully oppressive to white men, is a *luxury* to
them. " In Barbados, for instance, it is a great delight
to the negro children to place themselves at midday
on the limestone step in front of the school, in the
angle of a white-washed wall, and there to sit or lie
exposed to the full glare of the tropical sun, which
no white child could endure. But admitting the
objection of climate *to its utmost extent*, surely this
cannot deter us from missionary enterprize. Has
climate bound the extension of our empire, or of
our commerce? Some of the unhealthiest parts of

the African coast are studded with European agents of the nefarious slave-trade. If only as much pains had been taken, during the past century, to evangelize Africa as to debase her; if as many Missionaries had braved her climate, as there have been servants of Mammon there, engaged in the vile traffic of human flesh, ere this the Gospel would have reached the Kong Mountains. Had the same gallantry and self-devotion been shown, and as many lives been tendered for the extension of our Redeemer's kingdom, as have recently advanced the British frontier to the Sutlej and the Indus, no mountain barrier would have checked the triumph of our faith; it would have been borne victoriously from Sahara to the Cape, from the Gold Coast to the gates of Egypt." *

At any rate the fever of the West Coast is a very formidable foe, and is caused to some extent by the noxious exhalations from swamps or from the decay of rich tropical vegetation. The first symptoms of the fever are nausea, headache, and morbid fancies, together with sleeplessness and loss of appetite. The imagination is unusually active, but study is out of the question. As the disease advances, the longing to do impossible things alternates with a great apprehension of approaching danger. Then come fits of shivering, with dizziness, intolerable thirst, and, in all probability, delirium. To guard against it, a young missionary should be careful (1) not to sleep in the middle of the day—keep the mind active, do something during the day; (2) of course, to be moderate in the use of food, and abstemious with regard to

* Bishop Rawle.

alcoholic drinks—drink and fear have slain more white men in tropical Africa than the climate itself; (3) after a severe attack run out to sea, malaria perishes about three miles from land.

Apropos of the African fever a story is told of a slave-dealer, who shipped several cargoes from the Rio Pongo, that illustrates the blind superstition of the Mohammadan on the coast. The slave-captain on one occasion wanted to delay the start of a caravan which was going up country in search of a cargo. He was the guest of the Fullah chief, who was to lead the expedition, and on the morning of the start, the captain declared that he was suddenly attacked with fever. "I don't know," he said, "whether the worthy Mussulman understood my case or believed my fever, but the result was quite the same; he assented to my request like a gentleman, and expressed the deepest sympathy with my sufferings. His next concern was for my cure. True to the superstition of his country, the good-natured Fullah insisted on taking the management of matters into his own hands, and forthwith prescribed a dose from the Koran, diluted in water, which he declared was a specific remedy for my complaint. I smiled at the idea of making a drug of divinity, but as I knew that homœopathy was harmless under the circumstances, I requested the Fullah to prepare his physic on the spot. The chief immediately brought his Koran, and, turning over the leaves attentively for some time, at last hit on the appropriate verse, which he wrote down on a board with gunpowder ink, and then washed it off into a bowl with clean water.

This was given me to swallow, and the Mohammadan left me to the operation of his religious charm, with special directions to the servants to allow no one to disturb my rest."

Another source of anxiety and danger is, of course, the Tornado which comes with pitiless force and spreads disaster and ruin on all sides, undoing the work of long years in an hour's time, and causing sadness and sorrow in the missionary's home. A recent writer from the Isles de Los, thus describes it :—

"All is unusually calm and still. No sound can be heard except what is made in and out of the house. Even the birds cease their twitter. The air is sultry and we feel that there is a storm coming on. Suddenly it gets very dark ; the clouds are purple and lowering. There is a distant rumble of thunder. The island looks calm and dark, the sea is dark and unusually calm and looks dangerous. Suddenly a strong wind blows, and we have to make haste and shut all the windows and doors, because we know what is coming. It is comfortable to think that the roof is safe and not likely to come off. There is a vivid flash of lightning followed immediately by a terrific roar of thunder. The wind increases and the rain comes down in torrents. When we look out of the window no islands are visible. The sea is showing its dog's teeth, and the wind is dashing the waves against the rocks. It lasts for about an hour ; then the dark clouds disappear, leaving the sun shining brightly and the air clear and fresh. Just like an April shower, only not *quite* so light."

In spite, however, of both fever and tempest, Nature is kind, and compensates the inhabitants with some of the choicest scenes of beauty and grandeur.

As the traveller along the coast turns the prow of his boat through the surf, and crosses the bar that guards the mouth of an African river, he suddenly finds himself moving calmly onward between sedgy shores buried in mangroves. Presently the scene expands in the ruffled mirror of a deep, majestic stream. Its lofty banks are covered by innumerable varieties of the tallest forest trees, from whose summits a trailing network of vines and flowers floats down, and sweeps the passing current. A stranger, who beholds this scenery for the first time, is struck by the immense size, prolific abundance, and gorgeous verdure of every thing. Leaves large enough for garments lie piled and motionless in the lazy air. The bamboo and cane shake their splendid spears and pennant leaves, as the stream ripples among their roots. Beneath the massive trunks of forest trees the country opens ; and, in vistas through the wood, the traveller sees innumerable fields lying fallow in grass, or waving with harvests of rice and cassava, broken by golden clusters of Indian corn. Groups of oranges, lemons, coffee trees, plantains and bananas, are crossed by the tall stems of cocoas, and arched by the broad and drooping leaves of the royal palm. Beyond this, capping the summit of a hill, may be seen the conical huts of the natives, bordered by fresh pastures dotted with flocks of sheep and goats. As you leave the coast, and shoot round the river-curves of this beautiful wilderness, teeming with flowers and birds of gay plumage, you plunge into the interior where the rising country slowly expands into hills and mountains.

The forest is varied. Sometimes it is a matted pile of tree, vine, and bramble, obscuring everything, and impervious save with knife and hatchet ; at others it is a Gothic temple. The sward spreads open before you for miles on every side, while from its even surface the trunks of straight and massive trees rise to a prodigious height. At length the hills are reached ; and the lowland heat is tempered by mountain freshness. The scene that may be beheld from almost any elevation, is always beautiful and sometimes grand. Forest, of course, prevails ; yet with a glass, and often by the unaided eye, gentle hills swelling from the wooded landscape, may be seen covered with native huts. Such is commonly the westward view ; as far as the eye can reach, noble outlines of hill and mountain may be traced against the sky, stretching away to the distant horizon. At daybreak in the neighbourhood of a river, a dense mist will be seen lying beneath you in a solid mass, while out of this lake of vapour the tops of hills peer up like green islands. But ere long the " cloud compelling " sun, lifts itself over the mountains, and the mists which have haunted the valley since nightfall quickly dissolve, and the sun rises higher and higher in all its terrible splendour. Africa unveils to her master, and the blue sky and green forest quiver under his fierce beams.

" In an African forest," says Professor Drummond, " not a fallen branch is seen. One is struck at first at a certain clean look about the great forests of the

interior—a novel and unaccountable cleanness, as if the
forest-bed was carefully swept and dusted daily by
unseen elves. And so, indeed, it is. Scavengers of
a hundred kinds remove decaying animal matter,
from the carcase of a fallen elephant to the broken
wing of a gnat, eating it, or carrying it out of sight
and burying it on the deodorizing earth. And these
countless millions of termites perform a similiar func-
tion for the vegetable world, making away with all
plants and trees, all stems, twigs, and tissues the
moment the finger of decay strikes the signal. Constantly in these woods one comes across what appear
to be sticks and branches and bundles of faggots ;
but when closely examined they are seen to be mere
casts in mud. From these hollow tubes, which
preserve the original form of the branch down to the
minutest knot or fork, the ligneous tissue is often
entirely removed, while others are met with in all
stages of demolition. There is the section of an
actual specimen, which is not yet completely destroyed,
and from which the mode of attack may be easily
seen. The insects start apparently from two centres.
One company attacks the inner bark, which is the
favourite morsel, leaving the coarse outer bark un-
touched, or more usually replacing it with grains of
earth, atom by atom, as they eat it away. The inner
bark is gnawed off otherwise as they go along ; but
the woody tissue beneath is allowed to remain to
form a protective sheath for the second company,
who begin work at the centre. This second con-
tingent eats its way outward and onward leaving a thin
tube of outer wood to the last, as props to the mine

till they have finished the main excavation. When a fallen trunk lying upon the ground is the object of attack the outer cylinder is frequently left intact, and it is only when one tries to drag it off to his camp-fire that he finds to his disgust that he is dealing with a mere hollow tube, a few lines in thickness, filled up with mud." And again, the same writer's description of the White Ant may be usefully quoted here : " It is a small insect, with a bloated, yellowish-white body and a somewhat large thorax, oblong-shaped and coloured a disagreeable, oily brown. The flabby, tallow-like body makes this insect sufficiently repulsive ; but it is for quite another reason that the white ant is the worst-abused of all living vermin in warm countries. The termite lives almost exclusively upon wood, and the moment a tree is cut or a log sawn for any economical purpose this insect is upon its track. One may never see the insect, possibly, in the flesh, for it lives underground ; but its ravages confront one at every turn. You build your house, perhaps, and for a few months fancy you have pitched upon the one solitary site in the country where there are no white ants. But one day suddenly the door-post totters, and lintel and rafters come down together with a crash. You look at a section of the wrecked timbers, and discover that the whole inside is eaten clean away. The apparently solid logs of which the rest of the house is built are now mere cylinders of bark, and through the thickest of them you could push your little finger. Furniture, tables, chairs, chests of drawers, everything made of wood, is inevitably attacked, and in a single night a strong trunk is often riddled through and through, and turned into matchwood. There is no limit, in fact, to the depredation by these insects, and they will eat books, or leather, or cloth, or anything ; and in many parts of Africa I believe if a man lay down to sleep with a wooden leg it would be a heap of sawdust in the morning. So much feared is this insect now that no one in certain parts of India and Africa ever attempts to travel with such a thing as a wooden trunk. On the Ianganyika plateau I have camped on ground which was as hard as adamant, and as innocent of white ants, apparently, as the pavement of St. Paul's, and awakened next morning to find a wooden box almost gnawed to pieces. Leather portmanteaus share the same fate, and the only substances which seem to defy the marauders are iron and tin."

It is a great pity that no English traveller of modern times has penetrated this part of Western Africa, and that so little is known of a country which, according to the Vicomte de Sanderval, who passed through it in 1880 on his way to Timbo, is exceedingly beautiful, very productive, and occupied by an unusually fine and intelligent race of natives.

The people belong to the Susu tribe, and are of a distinctly negro type—black, with woolly hair and thick lips. They are tall and handsome, in this respect contrasting strongly with the natives of the Congo and South-Western Africa generally. The women are nice-looking and, what seems rather surprising, very clean. They are industrious, skilful with their hands, making their own clothes as well as mats, hammocks, baskets, wooden tubs, and chairs.

The Susu language is spoken over a space of 800 or 1000 miles, a country larger than Great Britain, and, in many ways, excels all the languages of Western Africa. In softness it even approaches Italian.

In the busiest time of the year the people are at their farms all day, busy planting their rice, fundengi, cassava, etc. They go through the pouring rain, men and women, young and old, down to the tiny babies on their mothers' backs. It does not hurt them— they are used to it. They plant rice according to the Eastern way of scattering it with the hand. Fundengi is a species of rice, a small round grain, and cooked like rice.

The form of government under which the West African negroes live in their own country is a despotism of the most decided kind. There is but one free man in a nation—the king. The rest are all his slaves, and he has unlimited power over their property, and even over their lives. The following anecdote of a late king of Dahomey will illustrate the extent to which this power may be carried. Being much troubled by a dream, in which he thought he saw his father and his brother, both of whom had been some time dead, he sent for one of his subjects, and addressed him in some such way as this : " I saw my father last night, and I fear he is not quite comfortable where he is—something disturbs him, makes him restless and uneasy. I intend, therefore, to send you with a message to him, to let him know how anxious I am for his well-being, and how glad I should be if I could do anything that would increase his happiness." The man's head was immediately cut off in order that this message might be delivered without delay. It then struck the king that, in his care for his father, he had entirely forgotten his brother; whereupon he ordered another subject to be put to death in order that a message might be carried to him also. The property of every one who dies goes to the king—nothing to the wife and children, except what the king may be pleased to give them. But though all the people are the slaves of the king, and thus subject to occasional caprices of the most fearful kind, their slavery is, in the main, of a very mild description. The subject is not required to work more than a quarter or half a day for the king; the remainder of his time is his own, and is found sufficient to enable him to raise food for his subsistence.

The slave-trade was first introduced by the Portuguese about 300 years ago, and Englishmen took a leading part in it, until, in the year 1834, through the unceasing labours of Wilberforce, Buxton, and a few others, the British Government abolished slavery in all our colonies, declaring the black man, in every respect, as free as the white. Great apprehensions were entertained lest the emancipation thus granted should, in the first instance, be abused, and degenerate into rioting and licentiousness; but it is a remarkable fact, and greatly to the credit of the negroes, that the day of the Emancipation was one of the quietest days ever known in the British West Indies. The first use they made of their newly-acquired liberty was to repair to the house of God to return thanks for the boon. We must not suppose, however, that because we have at length done our duty in emancipating

the negro in the British possessions, we have, therefore, done all that can be required of us; we still
owe him a heavy debt. What return can we make
him for 300 years of oppression? Surely the least
we can do is to strive to raise him in the scale of
mankind. And hence it is, that the cause of a
Mission to Africa comes before us with such great
claims upon our sympathy. Doubtless the West
Indies should be foremost in the mission, as it has
been for their benefit, primarily, that the negro has
undergone so much; but the inhabitants of the mother
country are, in every point of view, bound to lend a
helping hand.

In a pure Susu town you will often find a yard,
in the centre of which is a thatched building having
within it a sort of bed, or four posts with mats thrown
over them; near this stands a calabash of cooked
rice, a pipe or knife, and a jug of water, to mark that
a great man or head of a house is dead. They are
placed thus, believing that his spirit returns in the
night and continues the pursuits in which the man
was generally busied when in life. The very clothes
he wore are placed in this fetish-house, too. When
the funeral takes place a sacrifice is offered, frequently
a white fowl is killed and its blood sprinkled before
the corpse. Before the sheet or mat is wound round
the body all the family assemble round the corpse.
The head of the family takes the hand of the dead
and says, "Good-bye, you are gone. I have not done
you any bad (harm). Where you are going, remember
me." All the rest of the family in order of nearness
of kin do the same, saying the same words. After

this some words are said (possibly a prayer), and then
the body is wrapped in white cloth or else a rush mat.
The body, laid on cross sticks, is then carried to
burial, and, after some more words are said, it is
placed in the grave; over it, in order to protect it,
sticks are laid, their ends being fixed in the sides of
the grave.   Upon these sticks green branches are
placed, the earth is thrown in, and the grave filled up.
Some favourite possession of the deceased, such as
his sleeping-mat, or an old calabash, is placed on the
grave and left there, and there it remains, as no one
dares to remove it.   After a time the Kolungi, or
native feast for the dead, is held, where the relatives
can afford it, at which a sheep is killed, or one or
two cows, according to their means.   The friends of
the deceased are gathered together, and feasting and
dancing indulged in.   When Mr. Duport visited the
town of Yenungia in 1861 (Yenungia being a strong-
hold of devil-worship), he was horrified at the various
kinds of " *country fashion* " which met his eye in
every direction.   Mohammadan writings (*i.e.* charms),
natives greegrees, and, alas! the sign of the Holy
Cross, all mingled in a curious manner, hanging up
above the gates and over the doors and entrances of
every house.

The use of the Cross amongst them was thus
accounted for : " At the time when the nefarious
traffic in human flesh was at its height, Portuguese
missionaries accompanied some of the slave-trading
vessels.   These missionaries were accustomed to
baptize those who could afford to pay for their
baptism, and every one whom they baptized

received a little cross, which the priests suspended round their necks." * Possibly we have here the source of that knowledge about the Cross which some of these people have perverted to superstitious uses.

When Mr. L. Wilkinson's mother died at Fallangia, the female chief, Gomez, sent for the corpse (for the families of Wilkinson, the heathen name of whose ancestors was Tanu, and Gomez are related) in order that it might be placed beside the Devil's house, while sacrifice was made to him, and be sprinkled with the victim's blood, and then buried there. Of course Mr. Wilkinson would consent to nothing of this. So the poor woman was left, and, having descended from the verandah, Mr. L. Wilkinson, pointing, said, "That is the Devil's house." And there, in the centre and deepest shadow of four magnificent and stately mango trees, I beheld the horrid sight. I felt as if I could hardly walk, and could only creep, and I should think my own look must have been a horrid stare. I have no recollection of ever having been frightened by danger ; but on this occasion I was appalled, and from hot became suddenly cold. And my horror was increased by observing that a carpet of dark-green leaves, which was in front, was sprinkled with blood. I made, in three places in the sand, the sign of the Cross, and took possession of the spot, of the whole town and its inhabitants, in the name of Him that was crucified ! I crept nearer to the temple, and stooped down, for the thatch was brought down low— within sixteen inches of the ground. I beheld what there was within it. The house was like the dwelling-

* See also p. 73.

houses round, about two yards in diameter. There was an altar of earth, six inches high, in the middle of the temple, with bottles of wine piled upon and all around it, and a plate containing an offering of rice. With regard to the leaves sprinkled with blood, we learned that Mrs. Gomez had caused a bullock to be sacrificed to the devil. Its throat had been cut over the leaves, and some of the blood sprinked upon the altar.

The art of healing, as practised by Africans in their mode of dealing with diseases of every kind, is entirely different from that employed by Europeans in general. With the latter science is the law and the guide, but with the former the method used is just the reverse ; and, judging from the reasoning, and ways by which they try to effect a cure, we should call it natural and instinctive, or perhaps superstitious.

A schoolmaster at Fotobah, Isles de Los, relates the following : " I had occasion to hear recently of a singular manner of curing a sprained foot or broken leg. My informant was himself the subject of the cure. He is a native of Sierra Leone, and is carrying on a little trade of his own, among the Susus of these parts. ' On getting on board the vessel one day, by chance my foot slipped and I fell ; and in the fall either my foot was sprained or the bone was broken. In that state I thought the best thing I could do was to proceed at once to Sierra Leone for medical help, as I believed no one in the country could make me well ; but my friend, a countryman, told me that I need not do so, as there was a person among them who could cure my sprained foot if I applied to him. I consented, and made up my mind to try the country doctor, who, when he came, assured me that he could make my foot well within three weeks ; and that after this time I might walk about, or run or jump as I pleased. I was glad to hear this. But what do you think I judged of my doctor's skill, when he brought the medicines for the foot, and began to rub and tie them on the sound, uninjured foot ? Of course I instantly objected to this new and unheard-of way of curing a sprained foot ; but he told me to be quiet, which at last I was obliged to do. Soon the three weeks passed by, and I found myself perfectly better.' "

As to the religion of Heathen Africa, the negroes in the interior, it must be remembered, are not without a *kind* of religion ; and this religion is by no means found to be always a hindrance in the spreading of the Gospel among them.

Their tradition is,* that when the world was made, the Creator formed two pairs of human beings—a pair of blacks and a pair of whites—and that these four persons were the first parents of all the people in the world. In the first instance the black man and woman stood highest in the favour of their Maker, but, on a certain occasion, He summoned both pairs before Him, and showed to them a closed box and a roll covered with written characters. They were to choose between these two articles, and on their choice was to depend their future destiny. The blacks, being the favourites, had the first choice, and, impelled by that curiosity which is still their characteristic, selected the box, which they thought must contain something wonderful. They opened it, and in it they found

* Bishop Rawle.

nothing but lumps of iron, and lead, and earth, and clay, which they knew not how to use. The white pair took the roll, and found that it gave them a knowledge of arts and sciences, and of *the foundations of the true religion, and of the way in which to offer to their Creator such service as would be acceptable to Him.* The first use they made of their newly-acquired knowledge was to construct a ship, and sail away from Africa to a richer and more favoured country. The possession of the roll accounts for the white man's great progress in civilization, and the negro feels that the degraded state in which he now finds himself is a due punishment for the error of his first parents in not choosing the roll. They do not think they are altogether disowned by the Supreme Being, but that He has handed them over to the care of inferior deities. They do not pay—they think they have *no right* to pay—any adoration to Him, *that is now the white man's privilege* by virtue of his possession of the knowledge of religion imparted by the roll: *He knows more of the Creator, and may approach Him more nearly.* They may not know, and must not inquire about Him, but they worship the inferior deities, who are symbolized by lions, tigers, etc. They believe, too, in the existence of *evil spirits*, who, they think, have great power to do them mischief, and to propitiate whom is their great aim. They think that the Creator, being good, will not hurt them ; and that, therefore, they need only to pray to the *evil* spirits to deprecate injury. In front of their dwellings you will see what looks like a maypole, dressed with ribbons, beads, bits of glass, etc. This they call a "gree-gree," and use it as a charm to keep the evil spirits from injuring them. Some time since a converted negro explained how, before he had made up his mind to become a Christian, he had taken his "gree-gree," and set it up in a place where it was exposed to the weather ; that the rain had fallen and destroyed the finery with which it was decorated ; and, "so I thought," he said, "that if my gree-gree could not protect itself from the rain it could not protect me from evil spirits."

Into the subject of Mohammadanism generally it is unnecessary to enter. We are dealing, however, with a country in which the votaries of that creed abound in large numbers, and where polygamy is one of the standing hindrances to the spread of the Gospel. To refer, then, briefly to some of those difficulties which so often cross the missionary's path, and to give one or two instances of Mohammadan interest in the Mission, may be a fitting conclusion to this chapter, and help us to appreciate that self-denying and patient labour which must ever characterize the champions of the Cross.

"A West Coast trader" must have been a keen observer of what was going on about him to have written as follows :—" A journey into the interior of Africa would be a rural jaunt, were it not so often endangered by the perils of war. The African may be fairly characterized as a shepherd, whose pastoral life is varied by a little agriculture, and those conflicts into which he is seduced, either by family quarrels or the natural passions of his blood. His country, though uncivilized, is not so absolutely wild as is generally supposed. The gradual extension of Mohammadanism is slowly but evidently modifying the negro. An African Mussulman is still a warrior for the dissemination of faith as well as for the gratification of avarice; but still the Prophet's laws are so much more genial than paganism that the humanizing influence of the Koran must be allowed. In all the changes, however, that may come over the spirit of man in Africa, her magnificent external nature will for ever remain the same. A little labour teems with vast returns. The climate is not exacting, demanding but shade from the sun and shelter from the storm. Its oppressive heat forbids a toilsome industry, and almost enforces idleness as a law. With every want supplied, without the temptation of national ambition or personal pride, what has the African to do in his forest of palm, his grove of orange, pomegranate, and fig?—left to himself he will lead a life of self-indulgent indolence."

The Mussulman is never slow to argue that his creed is entitled to at least as much credit as any other. The Rev. D. G. Williams, of the Rio Pongo, relates the following :—" Because in some things Christians and Mohammadans agree, some of the latter conclude that both are alike. One of them said to me, 'As God makes everything two and two, *e.g.* two eyes, two ears, two hands, etc., so He has given us two religions, the Mohammadan and the Christian. We are both alike, correct.' "

And similarly : a Mohammadan Moonshee in South India once said to the present writer, " You have Jesus Christ, I have Mohammad ; you keep Sunday, I keep Friday ; I go to my mosque, you go to your church; I believe in my religion, you believe in yours ; you will not give up your religion, I will not give up mine." All the more worthy of record are those instances of Mohammadan interest in the Mission which occur from time to time.

On one occasion the fields in the neighbourhood of one of the mission churches were set on fire, and soon the loose grass was burning wildly. About 7 p.m. the church was in serious danger. " I sounded an alarm with the church bell," says the missionary in charge, " and in less than seven minutes over 200 strong men were on the spot contending with the rolling flames. The Mohammadans were conspicious amongst the valiant. Christians and Mohammadans vied with each other to save the church. Christian and Mohammadan young men scaled the roof of the church with branches of trees to put out the falling sparks. In less than twelve minutes the church was out of danger, for the crowd trampled out the fire. Amongst them was old Sori-Yarneh—the oldest of the Mohammadans—quite bent with age."

There, are however, two important particulars which prevent a good number of these Mohammadans from becoming Christians : (1), a firm and wholesome belief in the traditions of their forefathers, coupled with dread of censure in case they make a renunciation of their faith ; (2) polygamy, which is one of the principal creeds of Mohammadanism, and not tolerated by Christianity. This, at least, has been the missionary's unfailing regret, that they have known scores of Mohammadan youths and maidens who would have become Christians but for the two above reasons.

An incident in the experience of one of the Rio Pongo Catechists is no solitary example :—

"The Rev. S. Cole, myself (Mr. Vincente), and a Mohammadan were some time ago on board a Norwegian sailing-vessel which was in port ; and the shipowner, being hospitable, received visitors—amongst others, with ourselves, were a few Mohammadans who met us there. After due salutation we entered into conversation with them ; but the cleanliness, magnificence, and neat setting of the vessel threw them into a maze of wonder, and they were, as it were, forced to make loud exclamations. After a pause we interrupted them, and in our speech showed them the possibility of their making such vessels if they were only minded to do it.

"One of them, noticing the warmth with which we spoke, and having learnt that we were missionaries, entered into religious conversation, which we most gladly accepted. By his expressions we found that he was fully conversant with the historical portion of the Scripture—say from the Creation to Moses— as far as Mohammad wrote, besides, he was a grave and experienced man, consequently an *Alpha*. After a long controversy, he said, 'I believe,' speaking through an interpreter, 'that Mohammadanism and Christianity are one in essence, in that both serve the same God ; but what we Mohammadans do not admit, is (1) Jesus Christ as being the Son of God, (2) the Trinity in Unity and Unity in Trinity.

"In a long speech full of energy we showed him the base fallacies and fanaticism which exist in Mohammadanism ; this he saw as through a glass, but darkly.

However he, being candid, and as I had said, a man of experience, confessed that he believed in the Trinity. 'But' says he, 'I will never tell it to others, and you must know that all who disbelieve it—speaking of the Mohammadans—only know the Koran and other Mohammad books superficially. I say this,' he continued, 'because you are missionaries.'

"In proving to us the doctrine of the Trinity, he said, 'As man is a unity, but his unity is composed of three parts, namely, body, soul, and spirit, so I believe that God is one, but in this Unity is a Trinity.' Our joy for this man's simple confession of faith was unboundedly great."

The views of a modern writer are much to the point—*

"The resemblances between the two creeds are, indeed, many and striking ; but the contrasts are even more striking than the resemblances. The religion of Christ contains whole fields of morality, and whole realms of thought, which are all but outside the religion of Mohammad. It opens humility, purity of heart, forgiveness of injuries, sacrifice of self to man's moral nature. If, then, we believe Christianity to be truer and purer in itself than Islam, and than any other religion, we must needs wish others to be partakers of it ; and the effort to propagate it is thrice blessed—it blesses him that offers no less than him who accepts it—nay, it often blesses him who accepts it or not.

"The last words of a dying friend are apt to linger in the chambers of the heart till the heart itself has

* *Nineteenth Century*, December, 1887.

ceased to beat, and the last recorded words of the
founder of Christianity are not likely to pass from
the memory of His Church till that Church has done
its work.   They are the marching orders of the Christian army; the consolation for every past and present
failure ; the earnest and warrant, in some shape or
other, of ultimate success."

*The value of a Christian Mission is not, therefore,
to be measured by the number of its converts.*   The
presence in a heathen or Moslem district of a single
man, who, filled with missionary spirit, exhibits
in his preaching and in his life the self-denying
Christian virtues, who is charged with sympathy
for those among whom his lot is cast, who is
patient of disappointment and of failure, and of the
sneers of the ignorant or the irreligious, and who
works steadily on with a single eye to the glory of
God and the good of his fellow-men, is of itself an
influence for good, and a centre from which it radiates
wholly independent of the number of converts he is
able to enlist.   There is a vast number of such men
engaged in mission work all over the world, and our
best Indian statesmen, some of whom, for obvious
reasons, have been hostile to direct proselytizing
efforts, are unanimous as to the quantity and quality
of the services they render.   Nothing, therefore, can
be more shallow, or more disingenuous, or more mis-
leading than to attempt to disparage Christian Missions
by pitting the bare number of converts whom they
claim against the number of converts claimed by
Islam.

CHAPTER II.

The first missionary—Kennebec Ali—King Katty—The missionary's
hut—A wretched prospect—The old chief's sons' dream and story.

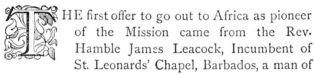

HE first offer to go out to Africa as pioneer
of the Mission came from the Rev.
Hamble James Leacock, Incumbent of
St. Leonards' Chapel, Barbados, a man of
saintly character, but already sixty years of age.[*]
Mr. J. H. Duport [†] (of African extraction) agreed to
become his colleague as Catechist. After a brief
stay in England, these two Missionaries sailed from
Plymouth for West Africa, and, after a stormy passage,
arrived at Freetown in November, 1855.

Mr. Leacock was much struck by the appearance
of the town, nestling in the midst of innumerable
tropical fruit trees and a perfect forest of exquisite
foliage, at the foot of the "Sierra Leone," or Lion
Mountain. Its fine streets, eighty feet wide, intersect
each other at right angles. Each house has a piazza,

[*] A number of details have been omitted.

[†] Of Codrington, and subsequently Battersea Training College.

with pillars at intervals, supporting a verandah that forms a shady walk, even at midday, and is surrounded by a garden. The fruit trees growing in these town gardens give the city a very picturesque appearance. Oranges, limes, bananas, plantains, guavas, avocada pears, abound everywhere, and afford a very grateful shade, attracting the sea-breeze from the wide Atlantic. On landing, Mr. Leacock went to the post-office to despatch news of his safe arrival, to England and the West Indies. Here, to his great surprise, he was addressed by name, and greeted with expressions of great delight by the post-mistress. She informed him that she had lived in the house of some friends of his in the West Indies, many years before, and that, as a child, she had frequently seen him there. This strange and unlooked-for welcome to the shores of Africa impressed Mr. Leacock much, and, in this apparently trivial coincidence, he saw the sign of a good Providence going before him and preparing the way. During his stay in Freetown, he received great kindness from the governor, Lieut.-Colonel S. J. Hill, who afterwards became governor of Antigua, and was for many years a warm supporter of the Mission. Mr. Leacock and Mr. Duport then started for the field of their new work, and on the next day anchored near the bar at the mouth of the Rio Pongo, 11th of December, 1855.

On the next day, the 12th of December, 1855, two well-manned and armed boats belonging to H.M.S. *Myrmidon*, took the missionaries up the Rio Pongo, and, turning into the branch of it called the Little Pongo, landed them at the village of

Tintima, nine miles from the bar at the mouth of
the river.

This was the home of the ill-famed chief and slave-
dealer Kennebec Ali, a Mohammadan, and, judging
from his behaviour afterwards, a man with but few, if
any redeeming qualities in our eyes. I must describe,
in Mr. Leacock's own words, the audience to which
our friends were admitted. " We were soon ushered
into the presence of the chief. Captain Buck of the
Myrmidon, who accompanied us, requested me to
appear in my gown, and, supported by him on one
side, and Captain Fletcher of the 1st West India
Regiment on the other, both of whom were in
uniform, I was introduced to the great man. In long,
loose, flowing robes gracefully descending to his
naked and unadorned feet, his head crowned with a
Kilmarnock cap, he received us with every outward
mark of respect. He invited us into the piazza of
one of his largest buildings, and desired us to be
seated. Then he wished to know our business, wished
to '*sabby* whether our visit was for war palaver.' Our
chief replied, with extraordinary gravity, 'No, your
majesty, our visit is altogether friendly, and has for its
object the advancement of peace.' He then told him
of my profession, and explained the object of my
coming. He stated that the English Government
approved of my Mission, and asked him to afford me
protection and encouragement in my work. But
Kennebec Ali was not inclined to compromise himself,
he only said, 'Nutting to-day! nutting to-day! To-
morrow palaver when de King come.' Messengers were
instantly sent off, and, the next, day at 11 o'clock,

Matthias Katty, King of the Pongas country, arrived, accompanied by his suite. A palaver followed, at which King Katty expressed himself willing that the children should be taught ; but added that he and his big people wanted no teaching. The crafty monarch was a Mohammadan, and knew well that the missionaries' teaching would require the discontinuance of polygamy, and this he would not agree to. Shortly afterwards eight Mandingo chiefs came in and asked for a private palaver with the two Kings, whereupon we could do nothing more with them, as they had been turned completely against us. After the palaver was at an end, I said to Katty in a private conversation, Captain Buck only being present, ' King Katty, I am come to you in God's name, to do you and your people good. I shall soon be alone with you. My friends who have come to protect me, will soon leave me, and I shall be then entirely at your mercy. Nevertheless, I am not afraid of you nor of your Mandingoes. You can do with me what you please ; I am not afraid to die, whether it be by fever or by sword. I am come with a message of mercy, to you and your people ; if you reject me and cut me off, I do not refuse to die —it will be better for me, for then I shall go home,' lifting up my right hand and looking upwards. How astonished was I, as well as Captain Buck, to hear this untutored savage's prompt reply, 'Aye yease ; but if we reject you and send you off, de gret God will reject we and cut we off.' I replied, ' Certainly, most certainly.' "

Kennebec and Katty could speak a little English and understand an Englishman who spoke " *in their fashion.*" Soon everything was arranged, King Katty signed an agreement, and then we separated. We returned to our boats, and in seven hours reached the *Myrmidon* still lying at anchor outside the bar of the river. On Monday, the 17th, Mr. Leacock and Mr. Duport left the ship, and again returned to Tintima, this time in a small and by no means safe canoe. On reaching Tintima the missonaries took possession of a wretched cone-shaped hut, which was allotted to them according to agreement. Tintima was very similar to the large negro villages in the West Indies during the days of slavery. There was no street, the houses being purposely placed in an irregular manner to prevent their being so easily seen by an enemy suddenly attacking them during the night. The cottages were all very miserable, generally circular, and having only one room ; the rafters of the roof were covered with immense cobwebs and black from the smoke of a fire made in the centre of the room to destroy the insects which were harboured in the thatch. Such was the new home of Mr. Leacock. It was not long before our friends found themselves beset by troubles, their first reception being a mere blind to deceive the British officers. They now met with every kind of discouragement, and were even treated with neglect and indignity. Provisions were withheld with the object of extortion. No one could be found to act as servant, and they had to manage as best they could.

Kennebec had retired to a small village near Tintima, and was ill in bed, On the 19th December Mr. Leacock walked out to see him, leaving Duport

to keep guard over their property. On his way the
guide enlivened him with stories of the tiger-cats,
wild cattle, and venomous snakes which he said
swarmed in the district through which they were
passing ; it was all part of one plan to get rid of him
again from the country. Mr. Leacock saw the chief
and spoke to him on the subject of his mission, but
with no result. He showed no interest, and made no
reply to any question put to him. Day after day the
prospect seemed to get more hopeless. Children
were promised as pupils, but not a single one was
sent. Two boys constantly lounged about the house,
and John Duport began to teach them their letters ;
but they were immediately ordered not to go to the
white man. Most patiently the old missionary waited
amid the very greatest discouragement, for the showing of God's hand.

At last, on St. Thomas' day, a canoe was seen
coming down the Little Pongo, and drawing near to
Tintima. A young black man stepped on shore, and
at once went to the hut occupied by the missionaries.
He introduced himself to Mr. Leacock most respect-
fully, and speaking excellent English. "Sir," he
said, "my name is Lewis Wilkinson, and I am a son
of Mr. Wilkinson of Fallangia. I bring an invitation
from my father, and an apology for his not having
called to see you before. He is now very sick, but
wishes to know when it will suit you to come to
him."

Mr. Leacock was himself in a state of great suffering, his face, hands and feet being sore, and swollen
from the bites of the mosquitoes, but most thankfully

did he accept the invitation. Leaving Duport at Tintima, to look after the baggage, Mr. Leacock was soon in the boat with young Wilkinson, and on his way up the river to Fallangia.

It is necessary here to go back and tell of a remarkable circumstance which had occurred a little before this time. Twelve miles above Tintima, on the northern bank of the Little Pongo, and by the side of a creek called Fallaniah, is the village of Fallangia, with a population of about 530 inhabitants. The chief of the place at that time, although a perfect African, bore the English name of Richard Wilkinson. Wilkinson was born in the year 1795, and was the same age as Mr. Leacock. Early in his life he had been brought to England, taught to read and write, and instructed in the elements of the Christian religion, in the house of the Rev. Thomas Scott, the well-known Bible commentator. On his return to his native land, in 1813, he relapsed into his former state of heathenism. In the year 1835 he was struck down with severe illness, and during this time, his recollections of his early Christian training in England revived, and he made a solemn resolution that if God spared him, he would pray daily that a missionary might be sent to teach him and his people the way of salvation. He kept his vow ; but the answer was long delayed, and now, in 1855, he had prayed earnestly and perseveringly for twenty long years, but still there was no prospect, apparently, of the answer which he so longed for. While Mr. Leacock was in England, preparing to start for Sierra Leone, early in October, Charles Wilkinson of Domingia, a

son of the old chief, had a remarkable dream, which
he told to his father the next morning, in the presence
of several witnesses. He said " Father, a missionary
is coming ; I saw him in a dream, walking from the
landing-place to this house." Old Wilkinson, in
common with the people of his race, was very superstitious, and placed great confidence in dreams. At
once he accepted this as an omen that his long-
delayed wish was about to be realized. When then
he heard, in the month of December, of Mr. Leacock's
arrival at Tintima, he was indeed filled with joy.
This part of our story points the characteristic feature
of the history of the Rio Pongo Mission, viz. that it
is Almighty God's own work amongst these poor
people ; His own gift to them ; His special answer
to the prayer of faith offered before His throne by a
black man, one who *had* known Him, who had
deserted Him, and who then for twenty long years
had knelt before His footstool as a true penitent.

To return to Mr. Leacock, whom we left on his
way with Lewis Wilkinson of Fallangia. One of his
letters describes fully his first interview with the
aged chief: "The old man met me, and, taking my
hand in both of his hands, pressed it cordially, and
before releasing it, said, "Welcome, dear sir, thou
servant of the Most High, you are welcome to this
humble roof." I attempted to apologize for having
come that evening. He said, "No apology, sir ; if
you will be satisfied with my humble board, you are
welcome ;" and he ordered supper immediately. He
seemed greatly agitated, and, a few moments after,
rising from his chair, broke forth with that incom-

parable song of praise the "Te Deum Laudamus,"
repeating it with great solemnity and accuracy. At
the conclusion, after a short silence, he said, " Sir, this
requires explanation." Thereupon he told Mr. Leacock the story of his life; his fall, and his long
attempt to wrestle with God, and added, "You are,
sir, an answer to my prayers. You are the first
minister of the Gospel I have beheld since 1835.
And now I know that God hears prayer, and that a
blessing is come to my house. Here you are
welcome. I know the misery you must have endured
at Tintima, left to the mercy of those creatures. It
is the most unfit place for a stranger in the Pongas;
and if you resolve on remaining there during the wet
season, you are a dead man. As you have come to
our country, I will find plenty of work for you. The
king of this country is Jelloram Fernandez; I am his
cousin, and my son is married to one of his daughters.
I know all the chiefs, and I will go with you to visit
them as soon as I am able. There are in Fallangia
over thirty children, which will be the beginning of a
school for you. You can use my house; and next
fall I will assist you in putting up a house for you to
reside in, and a place of worship. In the mean time
I will divide my house with you, and not charge you
house-rent. You can have a private table if you
prefer it; and if you should be sick, I will help to
nurse you." When Charles Wilkinson saw Mr.
Leacock, he at once told his father that he was the
missionary of his dream.

On Sunday, 23rd, Mr. Leacock began his work at
Fallangia, the pioneer station of the Mission. He

held service in the piazza of Mr. Wilkinson's house, read "Morning Prayer," after which the hundredth psalm was sung, and he preached on the words "My son, give me thy heart." The next day, Christmas Eve, Mr. Leacock returned to Tintima for John Duport, and that evening they were both settled in Chief Wilkinson's house, as his honoured guests. On Christmas Day, that great trial of the African missionary began to visit them. Mr. Leacock was attacked by fever, and was too unwell to officiate. On St. Stephen's day Duport was seized, but they were in the hands of kind friends, by whom they were tenderly nursed and well cared for.

Meanwhile one of Her Majesty's vessels, the *Teazer* had arrived at the mouth of the river, and her commander sent an officer to Fallangia, to inquire after the missionaries. Both were ill, and they determined to avail themselves of the opportunity of returning to Sierra Leone, for a short trip, in order to escape for a time the deadly influence of malaria. The fresh sea breeze soon restored them, and after a few days spent in Sierra Leone, they returned to their new home on the Rio Pongo, reached Fallangia on the evening of January 8, 1856.

CHAPTER III.

Mr. Leacock's warning—A witness for God—Requests for help.

THE attack of fever which drove Mr. Leacock to Freetown so soon after his arrival on the Rio Pongo, was to him a most serious warning. He could not help feeling that his life in Africa, considering his age, was, to say the least, precarious, and that he must strike quickly and do whatever lay in his power while his strength lasted.

On January 14, 1856, just six days after his return, a school was opened at Fallangia. Out of the thirty children then in the village, twenty presented themselves ; and not only children, but several grown men came and asked to be taught with the children. Chief Wilkinson gave every possible assistance. He told his people that he would not compel them to send their children to school, but that they were quite at liberty to do so if they wished it. "At the same time," he added, "I send my own, and shall be glad to see yours come." The result of this wise course was that the school excited great interest, not only in Fallangia, but throughout the country. The chiefs, although as yet for the most part indifferent to religion, were still anxious to obtain for their children (but not their slaves) the advantages of a good education. The prosperity of the little school was very remarkable, much to the joy of good Mr. Leacock, who, when referring to it in one of his letters, says, "May our heavenly Father bless and prosper this *His own work*. I know by this that many prayers are being offered for us." Such a happy state of things was not to continue long unchecked. On January 17th, Mr. Leacock fell ill again with fever, and was able to do but little for several days. When he began to recover, John Duport was seized with it. Still, in his journal, Mr. Leacock writes most hopefully : "I think we are passing from the Barbados climate into that of Africa very nicely. As exotics, we are doing pretty well ; we are gradually taking root in the soil, and hope presently to be as verdant and flourishing as any of the indigenous plants around us." With an earnest and persevering faith the two devoted servants of God toiled on, making the very most of the intervals between repeated attacks of fever. On Mr. Leacock this naturally told with most severity. He was really too old to battle successfully against such an enemy. John Duport, having African blood, youth, and a good constitution on his side, gradually became acclimatized, and with his strength, his zeal in the work to which he had put his hand increased.

About this time Chief Wilkinson's first wife (he

had five), professedly a heathen woman, named Martha, who had begun to take a great interest in Mr. Leacock, was taken ill, and one day when the chief went to see her she addressed him thus:— "Now you have got the *book man*. God has sent him to you. You must hear what he says: if you don't, it will go hard with you *to-morrow*." On my asking what she meant by *to-morrow*, Mr. Leacock said, the chief's answer was, "the next world." Not long after this, Mr. Leacock and Wilkinson were sitting together, when old Martha came in. Mr. Leacock invited her to be seated, and soon the following conversation took place, Wilkinson acting as interpreter:—"Martha, you and I are both advanced in years, and must expect soon to leave this world: what is your hope for the next? Do you know to what place you are going?" "No, I know not the place to which I am going; but my trust is in God. I never trusted in anything else, never in any greegree (a heathen charm), nor in any god, but the *great* God, from my youth. My father and mother died when I was a child, and from that time I have trusted in God." "What makes you trust in the great God?" "He has been good to me in feeding and taking care of me, when I knew it not, and could not take care of myself. He raised up friends for me." These instances show us that even among the heathen Susus, God did not leave Himself without a witness; and that there is some groundwork upon which the Christian teacher can build, viz. a knowledge of the one true God, and also of a future state, although it may seem buried amidst a mass of gross superstition and error. This they may, perhaps, have learned during their intercourse with the Mohammadan traders, or probably it is all that is left among them, of the teaching of early Christian missionaries. Even this small light seems, however, to have been fanned into a flame at once on Mr. Leacock's coming into their midst.

But the influence of the work was not confined to the immediate neighbourhood of Fallangia. On February 1st, Mr. Leacock received a very kindly message of welcome from Jelloram Fernandez, King of Bramaia, which was twenty miles south of Fallangia, and the chief town of the district in which Fallangia is situated. He thanked him for having come to live among his people, and asked him to pay a visit to Bramaia. He promised to send pupils, and to give what assistance he could towards erecting buildings both for pupils and teachers. In the year 1887, thirty-two years after this kind invitation, Bramaia was occupied as a mission station, under the charge of a catechist. The good news had sped also along the rivers far up the coast, for one day Mr. Leacock received a visit from a Greek, Mr. Columbini de Wasky, who had come 180 miles by sea, to beg that a teacher might be sent to his people—a married man, he said, for the people wished their daughters as well as their sons to be educated. He came with a Roman Catholic as a guide; and at the hour of service Mr. Leacock invited them to attend.

They both spoke English a little. The Roman Catholic declined the invitation, but Mr. de Wasky came. The piazza was crowded, and after service

Mr. de Wasky said to Mr. Leacock, "Sir, I have come from Cassini in an open boat, and had to encounter many tornadoes to seek the word of God for my people." He had come, as he said, from Cassini, or rather the villages on the banks of the Cassini, a river north of Cape Verga, between the Rio Nunez and Rio Grande. There he had heard of our Mission; and his father-in-law and all the neighbouring chiefs had deputed him to come and say how greatly they needed religious instruction for themselves and their children. What made this case doubly interesting was that *he was a Greek*, who was thus seeking to find Jesus. His touching request could not be granted, and with sorrow, be it said, the circumstances of the Mission have never yet allowed it to take up this work.

These two invitations from a distance made Mr. Leacock anxious to become personally acquainted with other parts of the country. Accordingly an expedition was arranged, and Chief Wilkinson agreed to accompany him. Chas. Wilkinson (Chief Wilkinson's son), the Chief of Domingia, fitted up his six-oared boat for them, a very comfortable little vessel, with an awning and a place for Mr. Leacock's waterproof bed. On Monday, the 28th of April, the two friends started from Fallangia, and were rowed down the beautiful Little Pongo to Mangrove Island, at which point it joins the Great Pongo or Sarnucha. Thence they ran up with the flood tide to Domingia, and finding that Chas. Wilkinson was away from home, they slept that night on board an American schooner in the river. The next day, as soon as the tide served, they started on their way, and leaving Devil's Island and the mouth of the Fattalah river on their right, in a few hours landed at Sangha, a village which stands on a creek running into the Bangalong. This was the home of a chief named Faber, a wealthy coloured gentleman, son of an American by a native woman, and one of the most influential chiefs in the country. Here they were received very kindly, and with great hospitality, by Mr. Faber. Not far from this, on the Bangalong River, is a ruined but once flourishing village called Liverpool. The name has come down from the days of the old slave-trade, and suggests the thought that possibly the great city of that name had something to do in former times with the trade between the Bangalong village and Barbados.

As Mr. Leacock was beginning to feel a slight return of fever, he rested quietly all that day, and on the next (May 1st), being better, they again went on their journey, and ascended the stream to Farringia, a town of 1500 inhabitants and the home of Mrs. Lightburn.

CHAPTER IV.

Farringia—The martyr of the Pongas—Samuel Higgs.

HE missionaries found Mrs. Lightburn a plain, humble-looking old lady, and were most cordially welcomed and kindly treated by her. She promised to allow Mr. Leacock to come and preach to her people. After two days they returned to Chief Faber at Sangha, who promised to give the Mission all the help in his power ; and then, on May 6th, they started for Fallangia, and reached home safe and sound. Before proceeding to tell of Mr. Leacock's last days on the Rio Pongo, it may be well to supplement this story of his first and only missionary tour on the river, by giving some extracts from the unpublished journal of a naval officer who visited Mrs. Lightburn at the very time of which we have been speaking. They give a good description of this influential and wealthy person, with whom the future work of the Mission was to be intimately connected. The officer was cruising on duty in the river, and says—

" We reached a schooner anchored off Bangalong at
sunset on May 1, 1856. Hospitality is a matter of
course among white men in the rivers ; I therefore intended to seek a lodging on board this vessel, which I
knew to be the property of one of the largest merchants
of Sierra Leone. I was delighted to find on deck the
very man I wanted—Mr. Leacock. I was struck by
his remarkable appearance. He told me that he
wished to reach Farringia that evening ; old Wilkinson was with him. Wilkinson must be very old—a
light mulatto, dressed in European clothes, and speaking English very well. They were travelling in a
commodious boat, fitted in the stern like a sofa ; but
in spite of these comforts I was much impressed with
the true heroism of a man at Leacock's time of life,
exposing himself to the risks and hardships of travelling and residing on a river noted for its unhealthiness, and for the purpose of founding a work that
will cost many lives in continuing. Boat-travelling
in African rivers is most fatiguing, and tests the
youngest and strongest constitution severely. After
a short time Mr. Leacock started for Farringia. Half
an hour's pleasant pull up the river (Bangalong)
brought us to Farringia, which I found to be a very
considerable town, laid out as usual in shady lanes.
Not wishing to disturb Mr. Leacock, who I thought
might be tired after yesterday's journey, I went first
to Mrs. C.'s, the wife of my particular friend the
consul at Lagos ; I found her up, but her daughter
was not visible, so I promised to call again later. I
then called at Mrs. Lightburn's. This most interesting old lady dwells in a commodious house surrounded

by huts and stores, etc., which form quite a village.
Standing on a large piece of ground, it is walled in
by a stout stockade of mud and wood. One side of
the establishment overhangs the river, the banks being
high and precipitous. I was politely offered a seat
by a mulatto who spoke good English, in a piazza
that overlooked the yard, in which was collected a
number of idle *Fullahs* and other traders from the
interior, all curious to get a glimpse of me. In a
short time Mrs. Lightburn made her appearance,
followed by a large number of female attendants and
three children, whom I ascertained to be her grand-
children. They were dressed in European clothes,
and had had some education. Mrs. Lightburn herself,
was dressed in strictly native style, that is, a large
cloth wound round the body close up to the arms
and reaching to the knees, bare-footed, and covered
with massive gold ornaments. In her hair which,
although woolly, was carefully dressed, she had a
magnificent gold comb. She appeared to be about
fifty years of age, possessing striking traces of beauty.
Her colour, although very dark, had a depth and
richness that cannot be understood by those who
have never seen an African beauty ; her hands and
feet would be a study for a most imaginative sculptor.
I had been told that she disliked English naval
officers, and therefore, although herself well able to
speak English, conversed through the medium of an
interpreter, which always renders these visits tedious.
I put, however, some home questions on the subject
of the slave-trade. She answered that she considered
that trade was broken up ; referring to the number

of traders that filled her yard as a proof that *legal* trade now fully occupied her time ; certainly a large trade appeared to be going on. I left Mrs. Lightburn in a good humour, having carefully avoided anything which I thought might ruffle her temper. An idea exists that she is not a slave-dealer ; such an idea must be wrong. She was married many years ago to an American from whom she has her name, who was largely connected with the slavers of the river. Lately she has given up her direct support of the slave-trade ; but her immense influence with the traders from the interior gives her the power of monopolizing any trade ; consequently she is one of the leading heads of the Pongas country."

Mr. Leacock reached home on his return from Farringia, on May 6th, thinking himself very well, but soon distressing symptoms appeared, and again he became unfit for active duty. The fever had now left him, but his strength did not return ; on the contrary, he felt himself gradually sinking. He proceeded to Sierra Leone in search of medical aid, and reached the house of his friend Mr. Pocock, on May 23rd, in a state of great debility. Thus ended Mr. Leacock's five months of missionary labour among the people of the Rio Pongo, whom he was now to see no more.

Shortly afterwards he was attacked with fever and ague, and in spite of every attention he gradually grew weaker until, on Wednesday, the 20th August, 1855, he fell asleep in Jesus.

The funeral took place the next day. The governor and staff, the clergy in and near Freetown, many

Europeans and natives, followed his remains from the cathedral to the new burial-ground, where Dr. Weekes, Bishop of Sierra Leone, read the Funeral Service.

The sorrow caused by the sad tidings in the West Indies, North America, and amongst Mr. Leacock's friends in England, was most profound. From all sides were heard expressions of sorrow, and of sympathy for the work. From the Danish island of St. Thomas, from Madeira, from Charlotte Parish, St. Vincent, and from Toronto (where committees were formed to collect subscriptions), from Madras, came the same encouraging message : "Go forward in the strength of the Lord God." From Fallangia, Chief Wilkinson wrote to Bishop Weekes on the 15th of September, thus : " After a lapse of time I have now taken up my pen, with a trembling hand and sorrowful heart, to inform your lordship of the great loss we have sustained in our beloved champion of the Cross, the Rev. H. J. Leacock ; and may the great Disposer of all events raise up many Leacocks in the West Indies to come over and help us poor miserable, benighted Africans."

A sum of money was subscribed by friends both in England and the West Indies for the purpose of erecting a Memorial Church, and in 1865, £250* was invested in the name of the S.P.G. in Barbados. In the Cathedral Church of Freetown a tablet still

---

* The estate into which this sum was put went into Chancery, and the capital sum became greatly reduced. In the present year (1900) the S.P.G. has generously given £500 in place of it, to be spent at once on church-building in the Mission.

recalls the memory of this good man, who was willing even to lay down his life for his Master, in the attempt to convert the heathen of the Rio Pongo from darkness unto light. In the parish church of Figheldean near Salisbury, a stained-glass window was erected in memory of the martyr and his visit to that parish before starting from England in 1855.*

The death of Mr. Leacock was, humanly speaking, a great blow to the Mission, which was now left under the charge of the young catechist Duport. He was, however, admitted to Holy Orders before the year was out, and on his return to Fallangia, he brought with him Cyprian and his wife, the schoolmaster and mistress engaged by Mr. Leacock just before his death.

The new deacon set to work with great energy to carry out the plan which Mr. Leacock had proposed to himself of building a church at Fallangia. It was begun at once, the foundation or chief corner-stone (of mud) being laid on December 8th by Chief Faber, of Sangha, in the presence of old Mr. Wilkinson, Charles Wilkinson of Domingia, his son, and William Gomez, Chief of Backia. The plan proposed was for a building 44 feet long by 30 feet wide, to be erected on a beautiful site near Fallangia, 100 feet above the

---

* The window cost £21 10s. In it there is a medallion representing St. Philip baptizing the Ethiopian, with the words "Ethiopia shall soon stretch out her hands unto God." "H. J. Leacock, of Barbados, preached the word of God in this church, MDCCCLV. An Evangelist at Fallangia, in Western Africa. He died for Christ and the Catholic Faith, MDCCCLVI. Aged LXII."

river, whence a view could be got of the Bramaia and
Sangaree hills to the south.

The day of the ceremony was a very memorable
one. *A great multitude* collected, and Mr. Faber
delivered a speech in which he reminded the
Mohammadans that they had done nothing for the
real welfare of the country, and that now the people
determined to follow Christ. After the corner-stone
was laid, the multitude exclaimed three times at the
top of their voices, "God bless this house."

On the day before (December 7th) Mr. Duport
baptized twenty-seven persons, and a month later
(on January 11, 1857) thirty-two more. On each
occasion all the candidates *were clothed in white
garments.* "The scene," says Duport, "was solemn
and heartrending. Many of them cried bitterly
during the whole service. Never shall I forget it.
The people in their white garments reminded one of
those who have passed through great tribulation, and
have washed their robes and made them white in the
blood of the Lamb."

Early in 1857 an offer was received by the Board
from Mr. Samuel Higgs, of Nassau, in the Bahamas, to
join the Mission. His testimonials were of the highest
character, and he seemed in every way fitted and
likely to become a valuable missionary. He was
appointed catechist, and reached Sierra Leone on
April 19th.

On May 11th, he started with Duport in an open
boat for Fallangia. The voyage was a most disastrous
one : for five days they battled against violent storms
of rain and wind, entirely without shelter of any

kind, and on the 16th landed at Fallangia, wet, and thoroughly worn-out. Their baggage was damaged by sea-water, and on arrival, the mission house was at best but a damp and ill-ventilated place in which to seek for rest.

Two letters of his are preserved, both addressed to the President of the Board, bearing strong testimony to the efficiency of the work which had been done. "I hardly expected," he wrote, "to have found the work here so far advanced. There is, indeed, a great work being done in Fallangia, especially in the school. The discipline of the school is admirable. There are fifty-two children on the books, and there is an average attendance of forty-eight. The congregation varies from 120 to 140."

But it pleased God to ordain that the hopes of the many friends of the Mission should be once more blighted. On the 8th of June Mr. Higgs was attacked with fever, the result of his exposure, and the hardships he had undergone. On the 21st he died.

Dark clouds seemed to be thickening round the struggling Mission, for on the 25th March previous, it had sustained another severe loss in the removal by death, of its good friend, Dr. Weekes, Bishop of Sierra Leone. His successor, Dr. Bowen, was consecrated third Bishop of the diocese on 21st September, 1857.

During this year the church and mission house were well pushed forward, so as to be covered in before the rains came in June ; and, on the 15th November, the seventh anniversary of the day on which the Mission was first proposed, the first church in the Rio Pongo was opened for divine worship, and dedicated to Almighty God under the name of St. James' Church, at Fallangia. In addition to his other missionary labours, Mr. Duport was engaged during the year in preparing a translation of the church service into Susu, and also a Susu primer.

CHAPTER V.

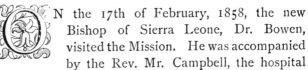N the 17th of February, 1858, the new Bishop of Sierra Leone, Dr. Bowen, visited the Mission. He was accompanied by the Rev. Mr. Campbell, the hospital chaplain at Freetown, and Mr. Black, of the Church Missionary Society. On the 18th the steamer anchored off the entrance of the sandbar, and the Bishop with his party proceeded up the river at about noon. It was after 9 p.m. before Fallangia was reached; but soon Mr. Cyprian was at the landing-place with a large crowd of people to welcome the Bishop.

Mr. Duport was at Freetown, at the Bishop's request, busied with Susu translations, and preparing a grammar and vocabulary of the language.

The Bishop's report gives his impressions of the Mission. "And now as to the mission-field of the Pongas. I look upon it as a hopeful one. A suitable European clergyman is wanted (*i.e.* English or West

Indian). I believe the climate is by no means so deadly as is supposed, with ordinary care, to men of fair constitution. Mr. Higgs fell a victim to the season in which he went down. What should we think of a person who went from Falmouth to Portsmouth in an open boat in winter? And the house of the chief in which he was, I do not consider well ventilated. I do not think I could occupy the room in which Higgs died, for a fortnight without feeling its effects. In fact I am delighted with the Pongas as a missionary post, and were it not for other works I have to do, should be very happy to occupy it myself, should the blessing of God remain on it. Where are the labourers? This was the first visit of a bishop of the Church to the Rio Pongo.

Two white men had now laid down their lives in the attempt to found a Christian Mission among the Susu people. Mr. Leacock was at rest in the new burial-ground at Sierra Leone, Mr. Higgs in the quiet churchyard at Fallangia; and in the mean while the work was being carried on by the young native deacon, Duport, with the assistance of Cyprian, the schoolmaster. More help was at hand.

It so happened that on 6th August, 1855, Mr. Leacock, immediately on reaching London from Barbados, attended a meeting of the S.P.G., and spoke of his intended labours in Western Africa. At that meeting there was present a clergman who belonged to a London parish, the Rev. William Latimer Neville. He heard Mr. Leacock, and became deeply interested in his work; an interest which was now at length to ripen into a devotion to it of his own life. An

advertisement was put forth inviting offers with a
view to filling the vacancy as superintendent at the
Rio Pongo. In less than three weeks four answers
were received, one of which was from Mr. Neville.
In his letter he spoke of himself as "being pleasantly
situated at Brompton, and in the receipt altogether
of a good income"; but having an earnest desire for
missionary work, he offered himself for the Pongas
Mission, "in the hope that he might thereby be of
service in promoting the glory of God and the
salvation of souls." Mr. Neville was a master of
arts of Queen's College, Oxford, having graduated in
1825 with second-class honours in classics.   For
twelve years he had been a laborious London clergyman—first, for nine years, in Bethnal Green ; then,
since October, 1854, at Brompton. He was about
fifty-five years of age, had never been married, was
of a strong constitution, capable of hard work, and
never so well as in hot weather.

In the evening of St. Barnabas' Day a meeting
was held at Brompton, at which Dr. Caswall delivered
a lecture on the Pongas Mission ; Mr. J. G. Hubbard,*
late governor of the Bank of England, being in the
chair. The vicar of Brompton spoke most feelingly
of Mr. Neville, and lastly Mr. Neville himself delivered
a most earnest and effective address, which brought
tears into many eyes. He expressed his admiration
for Leacock's character, and his hope that God would
enable him to follow in his steps. "But," he added,

---

* Afterwards Baron Addington, of Addington Manor, Winslow.
Sometime M.P. for the City, afterwards Lord Addington, and sometime Governor of the Bank of England.

"Mr. Leacock expressed his intention of laying his bones in Afric's dust. I have no such intention. I intend, please God, to live, and to come back from time to time to tell you what God is doing among the heathen."

So wonderfully and to all appearance so casually, in God's mysterious dispensations, is the seed of future good sown and nurtured! So strangely are the links of His gracious dealings connected with one another! On 6th August, 1855, Mr. Leacock spoke at Brompton of his intended labours in Africa : within three years a Brompton clergyman, then present, became his successor as superintendent of the Pongas Mission.

CHAPTER VI.

Mr. Neville at work—Africa for Christ—The missionary's home—
The Bansungi—The warrior chief—King Jelloram—More helpers.

EFORE the end of the year Mr. Neville found himself at Fallangia.

"It was a beautiful morning, and joyfully I stepped on shore," he wrote in his journal, "and if there was no human being to welcome me, the dear birds seemed to rejoice at my arrival, and to hail my coming; for kingfishers flew near me in various directions, and other birds flew round about me, and uttered a glad note or cry of joy. My baggage was but little, so two of the boat's crew picking it up, we trudged on together—the aspect of everything making a most favourable impression on my mind—till we got to the Mission station."

One of Mr. Neville's first acts was to examine the schools. He found the children backward, but with a fair knowledge of Holy Scripture. The number of *day* scholars was 101 ; of *Sunday* scholars, 106. The total number of persons baptized so far had been

173 ; and now, as the results of three years' work, at Christmas, 1858, a central station had been established at Fallangia, with a church and mission house ; the full services of the Church were being carried on, together with regular celebrations of the Holy Communion, which for want of a clergyman in priest's orders had been so long impracticable.

The Mission was now as it were making a new start forward, and in order that we may learn a little more of the character of our new missionary, it will not be out of place to quote here a few words from a letter of his to his friend, the Rev. T. Brutton, in England :—" I little knew the thrilling delights in store for me in Africa. I little knew what God had in store for me ; for I will confess to you I sometimes venture humbly to hope and think that He has brought me here. I cannot tell you how I love the dear black children in the schools. They love the white man that comes to teach them. In preaching to these black children I experience such deep emotions of love and pity when I think of their extreme and deep degradation as Pagans, and what they might be, and some of them are, as 'sons of God.' Oh, what a blessed work to be employed in bringing this people out of darkness into light! I never knew what it was to enjoy life before. Notwithstanding the heat, which is increasing every day, and the deadly climate, I am years younger than I was in England. I am as persuaded of the conversion of Africa to Christ as I am of the rising of the sun to-morrow."

The beginning of the year 1859 saw Mr. Neville settled at Fallangia and hard at work. His life must

have been one of very considerable hardship for a
man of his age; but still his letters and journal are
full of expressions of joy and extreme satisfaction.
He thus describes his new home :—"Approaching
Fallangia from the river there is an opening in the
mangrove bush, showing the way straight up the
ascent of the hill to the first stockade and gate into
the town. On both sides there is a rich broad fringe
of various tropical trees, flower-bearing and fruit-
bearing; and though there has been no rain for some
weeks yet, bedewed as they are by night, the leaves
—some of a pale (as the plantain leaf), and others of
a shining, though very dark green (as the leaf of the
monkey apple and locust tree), are all unfaded here.
Conspicuous are the rich scarlet flowers of the
titimindi, and two orange trees of the largest growth,
studded all over with globes of gold, and on all sides
shedding forth their fragrant perfume. On either
side of the gate, through the stockade, stand huge
trees—on the right a silk-cotton tree, with its vast
trunk, buttressed as it were by its strong and great
roots; and on the left a magnificent mango. Entering through the gate you see three great mango
trees, delighting the eye and affording a most pleasant
and refreshing shade. On the right hand of the
large space, stockaded as to its entire circumference
(in the centre of which are the mango trees), stands
the chief's house—mud-built, grass-roofed, and having
a deep verandah, brought down low, as some defence
against the tornado. But I must hasten on to the
mission house. If some of my friends in England,"
Mr. Neville adds, "were to visit the mission house in

this primitive place, and could see the way in which we are housed and living, I am sure they would smile, and allow that this *does* look like missionary life. The mud walls of my house, though white-washed and clean, are rather rough workmanship. In one corner of my room, the grandest apartment in the house, stands a barrel of flour; next to it a large packing-case containing books, etc.; on the top of it a gun-case; next in order is a two-handled saw about six feet long; then a great iron boiling-pot and the medicine-chest; then comes my large and valuable armchair; then a doorless cupboard, being nothing more nor less than a dirty packing-case turned upside down and divided into partitions containing dishes, plates, etc.; then a window, a mere hole in the wall furnished with strong rude shutters, window-glass being unknown on the Rio Pongo."

Shortly after this Mr. Neville went on a short missionary tour up the Fattalah; then to Domingia and Bakia, where he visited Chief Gomez, the brother of Mrs. Lightburn, of Farringia. He was a poly-gamist; but called himself a Christian, and said that he had been baptized by the chaplain of some Portuguese slave-ship. That these Portuguese clergy, coming to this place with slavers, did baptize, and receive as a fee a slave or two, is certain. In the rivers of the south, where the Portuguese had missions about two hundred years ago, crosses and "*Agnus Dei's*" are found in the possession of the heathen, and worn by them as greegrees and fetishes.

On returning to Fallangia, Mr. Neville learned that two days before his arrival the church, mission house,

and lives of all at the station had been in danger
from a band of devil worshippers. It appeared that
at about 9 p.m. on the day mentioned, it being clear
moonlight at the time, *Bansungi* passed by the mission
house. Three of our boys living in Fallangia, hearing the tomtoms (drums) and the cries, came up to
Bansungi and looked upon him. Now *Bansungi* is a
man dressed up in a certain way, who represents and
is worshipped as the devil. The pagans here believe
that, excepting his attendants, who have been
prepared by a mysterious preparatory initiation, no
mortal can behold *Bansungi* and live. If therefore
there is no house to run into, you must prostrate
yourself with your face to the ground. Now the fact
of these boys being alive some days after looking at
Bansungi was rather damaging to his reputation, so
he sent a band of Pagans to threaten destruction if
the boys were not given up. They wanted the boys,
they said, not to harm them, but to put medicines
and throw earth upon them, to save their lives ; but
probably their intention was to poison or make a
sacrifice of them. At once the chiefs of Fallangia
and Bakia came to the station, each with a band of
warriors ; meaning to act solely on the defensive if
possible, but at the same time declaring that if the
enemy fired a shot, they would fight in defence of
the mission station. At last the pagans went away
on receiving from Chief Wilkinson a promise of a
handsome present ; which he afterwards sent them.

The difficulty did not end here, however, for the
matter in which the three boys were concerned was
only a pretext ; in reality the invasion was a deter-

mined attempt to stamp out the Mission. Before long a large army of devil worshippers advanced again, under Simo, Chief of Yanungia, and occupied the town of Konfungea, about five miles from Fallangia. Several of the friendly chiefs assembled, and formed a guard round the mission station : and then, after causing many days of anxiety and trouble, on Saturday night, March 12th, one-half of Simo's army ran away, and he withdrew the rest ; promising Chief Wilkinson, as one of the terms of peace, that *Bansungi* should not pass near the mission house again.

During this blockade of the Mission, and at the time when an engagement with the enemy seemed imminent, a warrior was sent through the ranks to stir up the warlike courage of the soldiers—a custom which seems to be necessary amongst most savage races. Mr. Neville thus describes his strange proceedings :—

"Whilst I am writing, I am informed that a head warrior in full costume, with his piper and other attendants armed with bows and arrows, and beating a tomtom, is coming into the yard to practise fighting with an adversary. I did not approve of this ; but the next instant a gigantic African, armed only with a long sword, bounded in front of the room in which I am sitting, and instantly began fighting with an imaginary enemy. I am not equal to a description of his appearance. His helmet was made of the black-haired hide of some animal, and was like the 'bearskin' of our English Foot Guards, excepting that at the top it was square. From the

helmet in front depended a veil of scarlet cloth, about
eighteen inches long, with eyeholes, round which was
sewed white cloth, and the veil itself was trimmed
with an edging of black-haired skin.   Here I must
add that the black helmet had squares of scarlet cloth
upon it, and the veil, too, was ornamented with square
patches and wavy stripes of white cloth, and several
very small bells were sewn on to it.   He wore a
rather close-fitting body garment and wide trousers,
reaching a little below the knee ; both made of the
same material—native red-brown cloth.   Greegrees
(or charms) he had thickly strewn over, or rather
sewn to his attire, both before and behind.   His piper,
bow-bearing, and tomtom men kept close behind
him during his imaginary fightings.   He had two
tassels, depending by a sash from his side, with which
he wiped the blood from his sword, and little squares
on his body coat, and spots on his trousers representing greegrees ; besides this he had many bells fastened
to his back.   His boundings into the air, and the
leaps he made, pursuing his imaginary foes clean
over the mission fences, several feet high, were surprising ; at last he slew his adversary by cutting off
his head, whereupon he made a loud whirring noise
with his mouth.   Then he threw his head quickly
and violently forwards and downwards, barking like
a dog ; after which, bending forwards he twirled
himself round and round, and vaulted high into the
air.   Soon, however, another foe appeared, which this
time was a real living man, armed with a long musket
which he pretended frequently to discharge at the
warrior with the sword, but of course with no effect

—*the greegrees rendered bullets as harmless as paper pellets;* and so he too lost his head, by the sword of the invincible warrior. After all was over, he again bounded over the mission fence and away. I would not have given my consent to this exhibition, which was unchristian, savage, and horrible ; he came here, however, to arouse the armed men, who were lying in all directions about the mission yard and under the verandahs."

The work at Fallangia continued to prosper under Mr. Duport's charge ; the number of baptized persons having now increased to 205, of school children to 108, with 22 persons under instruction for baptism ; the average daily attendance at the church services being 80.

At this time information was received that Jelloram Fernandez, King of Bramaia, intended to come with an army to Fallangia, to burn, kill, and destroy ; and that consequently the Mission was in danger. Chief Wilkinson accordingly fortified his town by strengthening his stockades and setting up new gates. The Governor of Sierra Leone presented Mr. Neville with fifteen barrels of gunpowder, and a quantity of arms, as a means of defence in the event of the worst extremities. On considering the position of affairs, Mr. Neville now resolved on visiting King Jelloram in his own town, in the hope of making such explanation as would render him a friend instead of an enemy.

On December 5th Mr. Neville embarked in the mission boat, with a crew of four native Christians, and a heathen named *Pake.* Anchoring at the mouth of the Rio Pongo, they slept in the boat, and suffered much from great heat, combined with heavy dew. The next morning they sailed southward, on the Atlantic Ocean, until they sighted the Isles de Los ; soon after which they saw on their left the high volcanic mountain upon which Bramaia, Jelloram's capital, is situated.

The king was sitting with about thirty men in a spacious yard, adjoining his own house, and containing a temple erected for the worship of the *stone.* A long and unsatisfactory conversation ensued. Mr. Neville told the king that "as a priest of the Most High God, he had come to speak peaceable words, and to establish friendly relations ; " but the king was far too dexterous for the missionary, and it was impossible to bring him to the point of a frank disavowal of hostile intentions. He, however, permitted Mr. Neville to preach a short sermon, after which he rudely shouted, " When the world is turned upside down, I will believe what you have said ; but not before." At one o'clock, when Mr. Neville left the town, the heat was most intense. Entering his hammock, in order to be carried down the hill by bearers, one of the poles broke, and he was thrown to the ground and much bruised. On arriving at the water's side, it was found that the tide had receded, and the boat was aground. On account of the mud it was impossible to reach the barrel which was on board, and Mr. Neville endured the torments of thirst : not a drop of water having been offered him by the savage king. Bruised and weary as he was, he would gladly have rested on the ground, but multitudes of large red ants prevented him. A new source of anxiety was added. The king, considering that the same men who had brought up the mission boat might hereafter pilot an English vessel of war to the same place, arrested three of the crew, and it was only by the wise interference of the king's brother that they were allowed to escape. The tide having now risen, the whole party took to the boat, and rowed for their lives, apprehending an ambush. They toiled till midnight, and after a short rest arrived on the welcome bosom of the Atlantic at sunrise, and, in the course of another twenty-four hours landed at Fallangia, on the night of the 10th; but Mr. Neville was now prostrated by a dangerous illness, the effect of the unwholesome water which he had been obliged to drink on his voyage to Bramaia.

Christmas, 1859, was a gloomy time. The entire burden of the Mission had again fallen on Mr. Duport, who was distressed with the apprehension that Mr. Neville was about to be taken away, like Mr. Leacock before him. Relief, however, was at hand. On January 22, 1860, the Rev. Abel Phillips, of Codrington College, a deacon of the diocese of Barbados, was ordained priest, and Mr. Joseph Dean, a young English literate, deacon, for the Mission, in the Chapel Royal, Whitehall, by the Bishop of Barbados. They landed at Sierra Leone on February 12th, and arrived at Fallangia on the 17th. They found Mr. Neville still very ill, and confined to his bed. On the 22nd (*Ash Wednesday*) they saw him placed in a boat on his way to Sierra Leone, to be under medical care. The invalid was eventually obliged to go to Teneriffe for change of air, and was unable to return to Africa for several months.

Mr. Lewis Wilkinson continued to act as interpreter to the Mission. Writing at this time to acknowledge the gift of a watch which the English Committee had sent out to him, he says :—" We were once in darkness, and like cassava plants in a wilderness where there is no gardener, till the first preaching of the gospel by the late Mr. Leacock. Now streams are running into this mighty wilderness where the weary traveller may quench his thirst. The desire of the gospel is becoming great in this country, more especially among the *middling* classes. Our new missionaries were received with every demonstration of joy."

Mr. Phillips speaks of the good example set at Fallangia having its influence for a long distance round, even in towns hostile to the Mission, and of the increase of legitimate trade with Sierra Leone since the establishment of the Mission. On the other hand great difficulties still remain in the way. 1st, the opposition of Heathenism and Mohammadanism ; 2nd, the slave-trade, which is still carried on in the river, in spite of the vigilance of the British cruisers ; 3rd, the social habits of the people, which the prevailing custom of domestic slavery tends to keep at a low point. The commencement, however, of a new station at Domingia, and the acquirement by the missionaries of the Susu language, are matters for thankfulness, which may be noted in the work of the year 1860.

CHAPTER VII.

A dark year—The old chief's death—Another sad story.

 HE year 1861 may well be called the "dark year" in the history of the Rio Pongo Mission, judged from an earthly point of view. Its opening saw the young missionary, Mr. Dean, snatched away by death.

At this time, too, it was arranged that Lewis Wilkinson should come to England, in order to be trained as a missionary, at St. Augustine's College; but this was not to be, for on May 27th, his father, Richard Wilkinson, the old chief, died. This caused it to be necessary that Lewis should become deputy chief at Fallangia, under his brother Charles.

The following account of the old chief's death was given by Mr. Duport:—" He had a lingering illness, free from any very great pain. I went to see him a few days before his death, and spoke of the blessedness of those whose sins are forgiven, and whose iniquity is pardoned. He said he was not afraid to die, for he trusted in Jesus Christ alone for salvation.

He always said he had no faith in a death-bed re-
pentance, and on that occasion he added, 'and what
hope hath the hypocrite ?' On Saturday, the 27th,
I went to see him after evening service. I found
him in a very low state ; in fact, life was fast ebbing
away. I committed his soul to God, before whom
he was soon to appear. He lay like one sleeping,
as calm as possible, seemingly without pain, and
breathed his last at 12 p.m.

" The funeral took place at 9 a.m. on Monday, the
29th. The pulpit, the reading-desk, and the chief's
pew were draped with black. A crowd of people
attended, of all classes. I took the opportunity to
preach Christ to the Mohammadans, from the words,
' Be ye also ready.' There was scarcely a dry eye at
the grave. The people seemed to feel that the Mission
had lost a friend who could not easily be replaced.
The chief has fulfilled his vow, and ever been a
kind friend to the missionaries, while he served his
God faithfully unto the end. They were welcome
to whatever he had. He never failed to send them
meat when he killed any, and he allowed them milk
from the day of their arrival. Without him, humanly
speaking, the Mission would never have gained a
footing in the country. When open hostilities and
private stratagems were at work to overthrow the
Mission, he stood firm by us unmoved. Single-
handed amid all the threatened attacks of hostile
chiefs, and the underhand craft of false friends, he
erected the church at this place. Again and again
was he threatened with hostile invasion if he did not
cease to build ; but all to no purpose. He continued

the work, and has bequeathed to his sons and country-
men an inheritance which their forefathers had not,
viz. the possession of the Gospel. Immediately after
the funeral two heathens offered themselves as candidates for Holy Baptism."

One month later, and another sad story has to be
told. In June a new calamity befel the Mission
in the death of its venerable and learned superintendent, the Rev. W. L. Neville. The funeral took place
at half-past four, and all classes attended. A number
of Mohammadans came to me, and said, 'This old
man was a good old man.' His end was *peace*."

Thus passed away the *fourth* martyr of the Pongas.
While still thinking of Mr. Neville's end, two things
must be remembered, one suggested by the Bishop
of Sierra Leone, the other by Lewis Wilkinson. First,
that in a climate such as that of Western Africa, no
white missionary should be allowed to live in an un-
suitable house, otherwise his health must go. "Get
a good residence," said the Bishop, "and with God's
blessing, we may hope that men will be spared to
carry on the work." Secondly, "No one could
attribute Mr. Neville's illness and death (so said
Wilkinson) to our climate ; it was the effect of age."

Mr. Duport was now left once more alone, as in
1856 after Mr. Leacock's death.

During the later part of this year (1861) Mr.
Phillips visited Barbados and the other West Indian
islands, where he lectured and preached, doing much
good to the Mission cause. At Barbados he met
with an intelligent family of native people, named
Morgan, members of the Church of England, who

agreed to go to the Rio Pongo, and settle there as industrial missionaries. Morgan was a carpenter by trade, and had for many years been a master workman. He had known Mr. Phillips from his childhood. Mrs. Morgan was a most valuable housewife, who could bake, cook, and sew well, and it was proposed that the daughters should help with the school ; thus there seemed a reasonable hope that an immense civilizing power had been added to the strength of the Mission staff. This hope was not disappointed.

Morgan's eldest son was left in the mission house at Codrington College, preparing for ordination ; whilst Mr. Maurice, another Codrington student, was sent for a term of special training to Battersea College. At this time intelligence reached home that on September 24th the church and the old mission house at Fallangia (in which Mr. Neville died) had been accidentally destroyed by fire. Nearly all the mission property had been destroyed, but fortunately the new mission house escaped.

By the time that Mr. Maurice reached his destination, Mr. Duport had with great energy rebuilt the church. It was reopened for service on December 8th.

Notwithstanding the many calamities which had overtaken the Mission during this year, the prospects were never brighter than, through the grace of God, they were at Christmas, 1861.

CHAPTER VIII.

Rio Nunez —Strange visit from the Bansungi—Result of seven years' work—West Indian sympathy and interest.

ATURDAY, 11th of January, 1862, was a memorable day in the history of the Mission. It was the day on which the foundation was laid of the first church at Domingia, on the Great Pongo River, by King Katty, in the presence of a large number of people, and, as was reported, "amid the roars of cannon."

After this was done, and the new schoolmaster, Mr. Maurice, had been settled at his work at Fallangia, Mr. Duport started on a missionary tour up the Fattalah River, visiting and preaching in many of the towns. At the end of January he found it necessary to go to Freetown on business connected with the mission house; and while returning, the captain of the vessel carried him about eighty miles out of his way, to the north-west of the river, and entered the Rio Nunez. This was the first visit of any of our missionaries to this important river. For

three days the vessel ascended the stream.   The
banks were lined on both sides with the establish-
ments of French merchants and their Jaloff factors.*
Ropas, the town to which the vessel was bound, was
formerly a handsome place, and though at this time
almost in ruins, it still looked well from the river.
Mr. Duport was most kindly received by the resident
factor and his wife, the latter entreating him " to
intercede that a missionary might be sent them, and
they would do everything in their power to assist in
advancing the civilization and evangelization of the
people." On February 12th he left the Nunez, and
reached Fallangia on the 14th.   During his absence
Mr. Maurice had been ill with fever, but was now
much better.

One of the most curious events in the history of
the Mission for 1862 was a visit from the Bansungi,
or representative of Satan.   This is the person
through whose influence the Mission was threatened
with a hostile invasion in 1859, and who was afterwards grievously offended with Mr. Phillips, on
account of a sermon on the power and wickedness of
Satan, preached at Yengisa in 1860.   On Septuage-
sima Sunday (February 16th) the Bansungi most

* An important race of West Africans. They are an active, powerful,
and warlike race : the most comely negroes on the coast, having the
best features and the clearest and softest skin.   They are an industrious
people, excelling all their neighbours in the manufacture of cotton cloth
—spinning the wool to a finer thread, weaving it in a broader loom,
and dyeing it of a better colour. A distinction of caste exists among
them, and is observed as strictly as among the Hindoos. Their
language is quite peculiar to themselves, and is represented as poor,
but soft, and easy to be acquired.

unexpectedly presented himself to Mr. Duport at Fallangia, together with three others who were in the habit of coming over to church from Yengisa. Mr. Duport did not at first know him, and the Bansungi's own account of himself was somewhat marvellous. He said that " *the old people*," now dead, had appeared to him in a dream, and had urged him to give up *country fashion*, and join the missionaries. He awoke terrified, and fled directly to the house of a Christian, to whom he told his dream. At first the Christian could not believe he was in earnest, and sent him away. The next day he came again, and with better success. He was strongly urged to go to Mr. Duport, which he did on the following Sunday, and after some conversation with the missionary, attended the service in church. The congregation which had formerly dreaded him were now filled with amazement, some doubting his being sane.

Soon after this the Mission was still further reinforced by the arrival of the Morgan family from Barbados, on May 1st; whence they had come by a sailing vessel to the Gambia River. Mr. Morgan soon began work. He prepared a good piece of land for cultivation, with a view to instructing the people in the cultivation of cotton. The next few months were spent in missionary journeys from town to town.

Thus closed the seventh year of the Mission's eventful existence. The missionaries and teachers with one exception were now all of African descent. Through God's blessing the converts might be counted by hundreds, while the worship of devils and of idols had been to a large extent uprooted and abolished. England and the West Indies, for many years partners in the profits of the slave trade, were now in these better days associated together in the attempt to repay a portion of the vast debt due to Africa.

The visit of Mr. Phillips to the West Indies during 1861 stirred up a very keen interest in the Mission, which now began to show fruit. Branch associations were formed in Antigua, St. Kitts, Nevis, and St. Thomas. The diocese of Antigua during this year alone contributed £186, while £100 was received from Jamaica. The work only required to be made known in order to awaken the warmest sympathy amongst those who owned Western Africa as their fatherland. Shortly after this, Mr. Phillips, whose health had again given way, was obliged to comply with the wish of the Bishop of Barbados, who had recalled him to the West Indies, in the hope that his life, imperilled by frequent attacks of fever in Africa, might be prolonged in his native climate. Before leaving the Mission, he reported on March 20th that Mr. Maurice had been ordained by the Bishop of Sierra Leone, and now the work was once more placed under the charge of a single deacon.

During the year the duties of the two stations were faithfully carried on by Mr. Maurice. The church at Domingia was not yet completed, but services were being conducted by Mr. Coker. In October the good chief of Domingia, Charles Wilkinson, having promised to give up polygamy, became a candidate for Holy Baptism. About this time Mr. Duport arrived in London from Barbados, on his return to the Mission, accompanied by Mr. Morgan, jun., a young student of Codrington College, of African descent, and a member of the family already settled at Fallangia. From October 14th, when he arrived in London, until his departure for Africa at Christmas, he was constantly engaged in preaching or speaking for the Mission. In the churches of Notting Hill, and in many parishes in the diocese of Salisbury, he met with much encouragement. The pulpits of Wells Cathedral and Sherborne Abbey, and other great churches, were opened to this earnest black clergyman, who told the story of his African experience with extreme simplicity. His collections amounted to more than £400, the greater part of which was set apart for the erection of a new church at Fallangia, and to meet the expense caused by an unfortunate accident which happened to the mission boat whilst on her way to the Rio Pongo in September.

Many presents were given to the Mission, amongst which there came an ancient stone font from St. Peter's, Marlborough, which was afterwards placed in Fallangia Church. On December 24th Mr. Duport and Mr. Morgan sailed from Liverpool for the Rio Pongo, and landed at Fallangia on 6th February, 1864, " to the great joy of all the people, both Christian and Mahommedan."

Up to this time the number baptized (as nearly as it could be traced, for the first Fallangia register was destroyed when the mission house was burned down), was 421.

CHAPTER IX.

Fotobah, Isles de Los—Bangalong—Effects of American War—French
occupation—Want of labourers—Suspicious movements of slave-
ship—Occupation of Rio Pongo by the French.

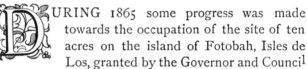URING 1865 some progress was made
towards the occupation of the site of ten
acres on the island of Fotobah, Isles de
Los, granted by the Governor and Council
of Sierra Leone. A survey was ordered by the
acting Governor, Colonel Chamberlayne, with a view
to making-over the land to the Society for the Propagation of the Gospel, in trust for the Rio Pongo
Mission. The death of the surveyor sent down to
mark out the boundaries occasioned some delay ; but
a "location ticket" from Colonel Chamberlayne con-
veyed sufficient authority for taking possession and
commencing operations. The S.P.G., with the view
of assisting the Mission, granted a sum of £400 per
annum for three years, towards the salaries of missionaries, and also (subject to a further report on the
climate of the Isles de Los), a sum of £500 for the
erection of a sanatorium and school there. The

interest which had grown up amongst the general public, both in the West Indies and England, round the work of the Mission, was now very great, and in Sierra Leone itself great interest in the Mission was shown, the subscriptions contributed by the inhabitants during the year reaching £50. In the autumn of this year King Katty, who lived at Tiah, and who had treated Mr. Leacock so cruelly on his first arrival, died of *delirium tremens.*

Two stations were now (June, 1864) no sooner in full work than the opening for a third and a most important field, presented itself : one, however, which was not to be taken advantage of for some years to come. On July 7th Mr. Duport tells in the following words, of a remarkable visit which he paid to the Bangalong :—" I am in great hopes of obtaining a footing at Bangalong next year. I have visited the place and seen the present chief ; he is inclined to give us a place near the town, but Mrs. Lightburn is our opponent. Bangalong is the town where the slave-trade was carried on in all its branches, and where John Ormond the incendiary lived some fifty years since. He burned out the first missionaries at Backia,* and afterwards shot himself. I have visited the spot where he committed the deed. It is an important place, and a key to the interior. There are several towns near, such as Sangha, Farringia,

* On Saturday, Sunday, and Monday 21st to 23rd of January, 1815, the settlement at Backia on the Fattalah River, under the charge of the Rev. Melchoir Renner, was persistently fired again and again, by the emissaries of John Ormond, each time that the flames were got under. At last, homeless and without supplies, the Mission was withdrawn.

Bacoro, Samucco, and others. I spent a long time with the chief endeavouring to persuade him. The morning after my arrival he called the people together and I preached to some thirty persons, from the text, " This day is salvation come to this house." The people were very attentive, and said to the chief after I had finished, that they were very glad to hear what they had heard, and that if the chief received the missionaries they would stand by him. One of the men grew eloquent as he proceeded with his speech. I left much satisfied, and am to return at the end of the rains ; meanwhile we have free access to the town to preach there whenever we can. I am the first missionary that has preached at Bangalong. All its former chiefs were agents of Satan."

During 1864 a hostile demonstration was made before the mission station at Fallangia, somewhat of the same nature as that which took place while Mr. Neville was there ; but as on the former occasion, now too, it ended in nothing. About the middle of the year Cyprian, the schoolmaster, who had worked at Domingia, Yengisa, and Tiah began to break up in health, and on August 18th he died ; at the last somewhat suddenly. He had done good work for the Mission.

As we have seen, the year just past was a very trying one for the missionaries, in consequence of the great unhealthiness of the season. In addition to this it was a time of very general and widespread depression caused by the American War, and the stoppage of American trade. This was felt upon the coast of Africa, as well as in other parts, as will be seen from the following extract from one of Mr.

Duport's letters :—" I am sorry to say that on account
of not being able to carry on legal traffic, the slave-
trade is being revived. The chiefs tell me that they
must live, and since no English merchants come to
encourage trade amongst them, they must take the
doubloons of the Spaniards. I am sorry to say, he
adds, that there is a slaver now in the Dubrica River,
consigned to King Jelloram." The distress caused
by the war was widely felt. Articles of clothing rose
100 per cent. in value, and food was extremely dear
in consequence of the failure of the rice-crop. So
many of the children went about the town naked
that Mr. Duport spoke to the chief about them, and
his reply was a significant one. " We want commerce.
The Christian religion, as it advances, creates wants
previously unknown, and unless these wants are in
some measure provided for, its progress is retarded."
In spite, however, of all difficulties the work continued
to advance and grow. The very aspect of the village
of Fallangia was changed by the influence of the
work which had now been going on for nearly ten
years. The appearance of the people, the condition,
of their huts, the town, the fields, the system of
cultivation, the habits of the converts, the church, the
school, the mission buildings all told of a great
power at work—the result of planting the Gospel in
that once benighted village.

In 1866 the French began to show a desire to
occupy the river. They first erected batteries on the
Rio Nunez, and established a colony there. They
then visited the Rio Pongo in a gunboat, and paid
King Katty's successor $500 per annum for anchorage

rights, expressing a wish to send a consul; the people of the river were against this, preferring an English protectorate, but the Sierra Leone Government took no steps to support them in their opposition.

The latter part of 1866 was a sad time for the Mission : on September 30th, Dr. Caswall, the energetic English secretary was compelled to resign, in consequence of continued ill-health,* and on the same day, Mr. Maurice's connection with the Mission ceased ; the cause of his resignation being the unhealthiness of the country. The chief missionary, again almost alone, wrote home to England thus :— " The Mission wants labourers. The work is arduous, the climate very trying, and the poor people benighted in the extreme ; I myself am not now what I was, the climate has left its traces on me. I need help, and that speedily." From Domingia he wrote on November 2nd, describing a terrific tornado which swept over Fallangia on Sunday, October 21st, almost wrecking the town. Later on, in the same letter, he thus describes the following extraordinary occurrence : —" There is much excitement here at present owing to the fact that a French merchant is reported (though he himself indignantly denies the accusation) to be engaged in the slave-trade. One of the English cruisers visited the place, to get information as to the truth of the report. It appears that the king of the Nunez, expecting a slave-vessel, sent messengers to various chiefs *here*, (whom he knew to be in the habit of selling slaves), to assist in collecting a cargo speedily, so that the vessel might not be delayed on

* His place was taken by the Rev. F. Bennett, Vicar of Shrewton.

her arrival. A few of these chiefs sent slaves to Nunez. This fact has come to the knowledge of the commander of the man-of-war, stationed between this river and the River Nunez, and he is now on the alert, watching for the appearance of the said vessel. When the king of the Nunez was remonstrated with, he replied, "Black men do not build vessels; white men bring them here. White men come to buy produce; white men encourage us to buy slaves for them; if it were wrong, why should white men leave their country and families, and risk their lives to do it? Oh no! as long as white men come to buy, so long we must supply them!"

On St. Andrew's Day (Sunday) an officer from a French steamer which had just anchored in the river off Domingia, announced to us that he was commissioned by the governor of Senegal, to inform the missionary that the French had taken possession of the Rio Pongo, for the purpose of forwarding civilization, and that the governor would like to know something of the missionaries and their work. He inspected the church, school, and mission premises.

CHAPTER X.

HE end of the year 1866 found Mr. Duport once more practically alone, in charge of the Mission. Mr. Maurice and Mr. Morgan, jun., had both retired during the year, on the ground of the unhealthiness of the country. Happily, however, the staff was again materially strengthened by the arrival, on June 22nd, of Messrs. J. F. Turpin and P. H. Doughlin from Barbados. They were both students of Codrington College, and men of great promise. The former had been employed for some months as a reader and catechist in St. Vincent, amongst the Caribs, under the direction of the Rev. G. M. D. Frederick (afterwards Archdeacon of Barbados). Both suffered severely from African fever on their first arrival.

At this time the French Government took formal possession of the Rio Pongo, "for the protection of trade, and the advancement of civilization," and placed it under the commandant of Senegal.

At the close of 1867 the staff was as follows : — Rev. J. H. A. Duport, in charge ; Mr. Turpin, catechist at Domingia ; Mr. Doughlin, catechist at Fallangia ; Mr. W. S. Macaulay, catechist and schoolmaster at Fotobah ; Mr. E. E. Bickersteth, schoolmaster at Fallangia ; and two schoolmistresses, one at Domingia, and one at Fallangia.

In 1868 Mr. Turpin was ordained Deacon on the fourth Sunday in Advent (December 20th), and Mr. Doughlin was preparing himself for ordination. Both of them made good progress during the year in acquiring the Susu language. The Isles de Los station had begun to bear fruit, and very great hopes were entertained that it might, in the course of time, become not merely a sanatorium, but the Iona of the Mission. The number of baptisms during the year 1868 was 51, making the total number of persons baptized since the commencement of the Mission at Christmas, 1855, by the West Indian missionaries, 537. The number of communicants increased during the year from 40 to 53, and at its close there were 28 candidates for Holy Baptism and 80 for Confirmation.

In 1869 Mr. Duport and his family sailed on May 3rd for the Rio Nunez, the Governor of Senegal having given his permission for him to open a station there. The shores of this river near the mouth are occupied by a wild tribe called the Bagas, whom Mr. Duport described as the most degraded savages he had seen in Africa. The king and the population of the upper river are Nalloos, a more independent and

a finer race, apparently, than even the Mulattos of the
Rio Pongo. At a meeting of the king and chiefs at
Kannsup, it was decided that three buildings should
be erected in Kanfarandey, at a place called Gem-
masansan (Gemme St. Jean) *the foot of rocks*, consist-
ing of a church and school under one roof, a dwelling-
house for the missionary, of the same size as that at
Domingia, and a residence for children from a distance.
The majority of the people speak or understand the
Susu language, this being the trade language of the
coast from Sierra Leone northwards, wherever regular
trade is carried on; English, too, is understood a
little by many of the chiefs who were trained under
English masters in days gone by. Why Englishmen left the river finally cannot be satisfactorily
ascertained.

CHAPTER XI.

N the beginning of the year 1870 the work of the Mission was going forward at four centres. Fallangia, the original station on the little Pongo, where there were two mission houses and a church with outposts at Backia, Yengisa and Sangui, under Mr. P. H. Doughlin, catechist, with Mr. Macauley, school-master; Domingia, an important trading-place on the Great Pongo, with a church and mission-house newly erected by the Mulatto chiefs, under the acting chief missionary, Rev. D. G. Williams, with Mr. Bickersteth as schoolmaster, who worked the outposts at Kissin, Lokatah, and Xundiyeri; Fotobah, on the Isles de Los, midway between the Rio Pongo and Sierra Leone, with outposts at Boom and Rogbana on the same island, Cassa on Factory Island, and the settlement on Crawford island, under the charge of the Rev. J. F. Turpin; Gemme St. Jean, on the Rio

Nunez, 100 miles north of the Rio Pongo.   Here the
Rev. J. H. Duport was working, on the invitation of
Gura Tasol, the Mohammadan king of the Naloos.
The reports received from the stations, as well as
those of the acting superintendant, tell of steady pro-
gressive work, the two stations of Domingia and
Fallangia being now fully provided for, and well looked
after by Mr. Doughlin, whose energy was untiring.
The report tells us that in order to press the people
to come in to his weekday evening services, he
adopted the plan of St. Francis Xavier, who walked
through the streets of Goa, with a bell in his hand,
summoning all masters for the love of God, to send
their children and slaves to be catechized.

The Mission was now to suffer a great loss in the
removal from this world of one of its founders and
chief fathers, Bishop Parry of Barbados, the first
president of the mission board.   He died at West
Malvern, on Wednesday, 16th March, 1870, in the
seventy-sixth year of his age.

On May 12th, the Rev. Prebendary Bennett resigned
the post of Hon. Sec. to the English Committee of the
Mission, and his place was taken by the Rev. A. Reece,
vicar of Withiel Florey.   While these changes in the
Executive Committee at home were taking place,
discouraging accounts began to arrive from Mr.
Turpin of the work in the Isles de Los.   The love of
some was beginning to wax cold, and the consequent
results, neglect and indifference, began to appear.
Even among the new church-goers the novelty was
wearing off, and indifference to good could not last
long without the inevitable development of evil.

During a visit which Mr. Turpin was compelled to pay to Freetown, a *Simoi ceremony* was held in the town. This is the kind of devil worship held in memory of the dead. Far out in the bush sacrifices are offered ; a cake is prepared from rice-flour, and placed on a large stone. The people first kneel round it and pray, after which they dance round in a most indecent manner, to the sound of the drum. The family of the dead persons then eat of the cake and become members (of Simo); afterwards, in many instances, having their teeth filed. This Simoi festival was held in memory of the mother of a young woman who was a native of Boom ; the mother had died, about a year before in Sierra Leone. People came to the feast, which was kept up with the usual drumming, dancing, and firing of guns from Boom Cassa, and the mainland. Amongst the members were some of the baptized Christians who had allowed their curiosity and love of excitement to overcome them.

At the beginning of January, 1871, Mr. Duport left his station on the Rio Nunez for a short visit to Sierra Leone, and whilst on his return home, was met with the painful intelligence that the whole mission premises at Gemme St. Jean were destroyed by fire on Sunday, January 15th, just twelve days after he had left. Nothing was saved, and Mr. Duport's family was houseless and destitute. The fire broke out at seven o'clock in the evening ; one of the schoolboys accidentally lighted the grass, from which the fire spread to the buildings. All Mr. Duport's books, presents received in England and the West Indies—among which was a

private Communion service—everything of value that
he had, was gone. Of the three buildings, nothing
remained. It was a terrible blow, and for a time Mr.
Duport seemed quite crushed down by it. The sympathy, however, that he received from the native chiefs
and English and French merchants, both on the Rio
Nunez and Rio Pongo, inspired him with new zeal. His
friends came forward and helped him with money so
kindly that, in six months after the fire, he was able
to remove with his family into a new mission house,
and within ten months to witness the dedication of
the new church.

During the year 1871 the reports told of steady
work at all the stations, although the Mission was
short-handed. A new Bishop of Sierra Leone, now
arrived from England—Dr Cheetham—who, by the
wish of the Board, sent for our two missionaries, and
on October 22nd, ordained Mr. Turpin a priest, and
admitted Mr. Doughlin to deacon's orders. The
two newly-ordained missionaries returned to the Rio
Pongo with the Rev. D. G. Williams, who was still
visiting superintendent of the Mission, and, after
spending a Sunday at Domingia, the Revs. D. G.
Williams and J. F. Turpin went on to the Rio Nunez
to assist Mr. Duport at the opening of his new church.
The work had been thoroughly done. The ground plan
of the church was cruciform, and to it was attached a
fireproof vestry in which the books, registers, etc.,
would be kept.

On the return of Messrs. Williams and Turpin, they
found that a new helper had arrived at Fotobah ; this
was the Rev. J. B. McEwen, who, after a short stay

at Fotobah, was sent to Fallangia to relieve Mr. Doughlin, and set him free to devote all his energy to the work at Domingia. Thus, at the end of 1871, after many great causes for discouragement, the Mission staff was once more built up, and the work prospering. God was still with his servants, who were battling on amid great difficulties, in this most trying part of His Mission field.

CHAPTER XII.

"Simoi" bushes—Mr. Duport's illness and death—Missionary tours—
Conference.

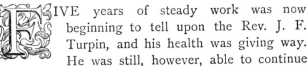

IVE years of steady work was now beginning to tell upon the Rev. J. F. Turpin, and his health was giving way. He was still, however, able to continue his regular duties during the first half-year of 1872. He then left for a trip to the West Indies and England for the sake of his health.

From Mr. Doughlin at Domingia came the sad news that during the early part of this year *Simoi bushes* had been established in various heathen towns about the country, for the purpose of admitting people into the dread mysteries of heathenism, in opposition to the efforts of the Mission. This struck terror into the hearts of all, especially those who had to travel. There were two of these bushes on the road from Fallangia to Domingia by land, and one at Kaninjla opposite to Fallangia, on the other side of the river. Usually notice is given of the intention to stick *Simo* in a particular spot, and a peculiar drumming is kept up there, during *the dancing of the Sons of Simo.* Those who wish to join, enter the bush and remain there for six months. During the first three they are said to be dead. They are washed and brought back to life, taught the songs, language, dances, etc., of the *Simoi,* and come out with dreadful scars on their backs—signs of the treatment they have met with—so dreadful indeed, that " *Simo sofo* " (to stick Simo) is proverbial for undergoing any painful operation. It is customary to set bounds round these bushes, beyond which none but the initiated are allowed to pass with impunity. Should any male pass them unawares, he must eat the *Simo,* that is, join their people, or else redeem himself with a great sum of money. For a woman there is no alternative but death. How true is it, indeed, that " *the dark places of the earth are full of the habitations of cruelty."* In spite of this there was much cause for thankfulness and encouragement in the steady though slow growth of the work at the stations. Very interesting cases were reported from time to time. One is that of a woman named Saio, who, about four years back, exposed her child to death in the bush, saying that it was a witch, and inquired if there were no piazzas attached to heaven for such as had a desire for happiness, but could not trouble themselves with the duties of religion. She now became a catechumen and began to attend church. In the same class with her were two men, who were formerly Mohammadans. Another who joined the class was a woman named Maninga, who, on one occasion, swept her house and threw the dust on the late Mr. Morgan, as he was speaking to her and urging her to become a Christian. Shortly before joining she said that her idea of the way to get to heaven was to give. "If you give," she said, "you will go to heaven. If you don't give you will not go there." It was, however, and always has been a drawback, that the mission staff being short-handed, the missionaries are obliged to be away a great deal from their stations itinerating from village to village.

In 1872 the Bishop of Sierra Leone visited the Isles de Los, and confirmed twenty-one persons, this being the first Confirmation ever held on the islands. At the end of the year the Fallangia registers showed that during the past seventeen years, 571 persons had been admitted to Holy Baptism at that station, 80 adults had been confirmed, 14 couples had sought God's blessing in Holy Matrimony, and 65 persons had been laid in the grave with the rites of Christian burial. At Domingia during eleven years, there had been 236 baptisms, 7 marriages, and 19 funerals, making in all a total at these stations of 807 baptisms, 21 marriages, and 84 funerals. Tables and numbers can give but a poor estimate of the time, labour, and money expended, and they give no idea of the trials and disappointments experienced ; still, however, it is very necessary that they should be kept, and recorded occasionally.

Notwithstanding his bad state, of health Mr. Duport, during his stay on the Rio Pongo, preached three times at Domingia and four times at Fallangia ;

administered the Holy Communion three times at the former place, and four times at the latter, besides helping as far as he was able in the services. This was the last work he was to do for the Mission, for it was now considered quite necessary that he should go home to England, to seek, if possible, the restoration of his health ; but this, as it proved, was not to be. He died on September 20th and was buried at St. James' Cemetery, Liverpool.

When the end was near, he said that, on reviewing his past life, he could not but wonder at his great presumption in ever becoming a minister of the Gospel. The responsibility seemed so great, that he wondered at any one accepting it, and trembled at the thought. It was only on the mercy and merits of Him Who had laid such a responsibility upon him, that he could place any trust.

The Day of Intercession was observed in 1873 on December 3rd, and was sadly clouded over by the news of Mr. Duport's death. As soon as the people heard of it they flocked to the mission house to sympathize with the clergy. On December 11th, Mr. McEwen started on a missionary tour up the Dubrika River, and the following notes of his journey give to us a very interesting account of the country in the neighbourhood of Bramaia.

" We landed first at Conakry, the nearest point to these islands. The very first thing that met our view, and invariably did so at each place where we landed, was an idol or devil's house, beneath a large silk-cotton tree near the beach. Strange to say, we found on the side of the tree nearest to this settlement, a Latin

cross distinctly carved out, which had apparently
been there for many years, perhaps cut by one of the
early missionaries of the Church Missionary Society.
Hence we walked across to Bullabina, another small
town.   Both chiefs were glad to see us.   The same
day we started up the river, and, the wind being fair,
we reached Kapparoo, the residence of King Demba,
at 5 p.m. ; we called upon him, and he made his
attendants at once bring cola, the customary present,
signifying goodwill and friendship.   We slept at
Kapparoo that night.   Here the C.M.S. had a school
about fifty years ago, but now there is no trace of it,
nor of those who were brought up in it.   Most of the
people follow the Mahommedan creed.   Kapparoo is
a good specimen of an African town ; the houses,
although built of the usual country materials, are far
more substantial than the houses on the Rio Pongo,
shewing more pains and skill in their construction.
There was the regular court-house by itself in the
centre of the town, where the King and chiefs meet
to settle great matters.   There was the mosque not
far from it, where at five in the morning, and six in
the evening, they gather to pray.   The worshippers
were not pretenders ; but among them were some
venerable-looking old men, whose earnestness and
evident purity of heart, were well worthy of the best
religion.   The Isles de Los were formerly the
possession of the kings of Kapparoo.   The next
morning we proceeded on our journey, and by midday
we had sailed fairly into the Dubrika River, and left
the sea-coast altogether.   We reached the town of
Dubrika at half-past four, and as soon as we landed

went to see the chief Sookbe, who at once made us feel at home. At sunset we walked out of the town into the open country to have a sight of the high mountain which we had been admiring all the way up. We slept at the chief's house, and next day starting with the early tide for Corera, we arrived there about two o'clock. Here we felt that we were no longer near the sea, but far inland, and the prospect around us was an unusual one. We were now ninety miles from the Isles de Los, and the high mountain peaks and hills were close to us. Here the bamboo grew luxuriantly, and the river-water, unlike the muddy-looking colour of the branches near the sea, was as clear as possible. Bocary Bango was chief of Corera, and his country embraced a large tract of territory. The town is on elevated ground— —indeed the whole country is, and the climate is very pleasant and cool. The old chief, who lived in patriarchal style, with his sons, received us warmly. Every morning his sons and people, as soon as they are up, go to him to pay their respects by making obeisance to him. The chief's sons accompanied us through the town, which was a large one, to the top of one of the high hills near, whence we had a splendid view of the whole country round. The day after our arrival was Sunday, and we held service in the Piazza, which was attended by a large number of natives as well as the chief's sons. Bocary Bango is of pure Susu race, and at Corera the Susu language is spoken much purer than near the sea-coasts. On the fourth day after our arrival we returned home- wards ; the old chief expressing great pleasure at our visit. On the way down we landed at several towns and villages, and reached home safely on December 18th, glad and thankful to find that Mr. Turpin and his sister had arrived from England. The Christmas of 1873 was a bright and happy one."

In the autumn of 1874 the staff was recruited by the arrival from Barbados of the Rev. R. J. Clarke, ordained deacon before his departure for work in the Mission. In November a Conference of the missionaries was held at Domingia. This was followed by public meetings, which stirred up considerable interest, and were largely attended by influential natives, some of whom were heathen, others Mohammadans. At Fallangia the chair was taken by Mr. Curtis, the prime minister. The following speeches made at the meeting are worthy of preservation :—

After several chiefs had spoken, Mr. Demba got up and said, "I am a Mohammadan. I feel that the Christian religion has brought great blessings to this country. I am a young man, but I would ask the old people which of them can remember nineteen years to have passed without war in this country. There has been no war now for more than nineteen years, and this is the result of the Christian religion. It is our privilege to live in the peace of the Gospel ; let us shew that we value these privileges. The Mission has given us feet to walk with ; we must now begin to use our hands. Mohammadans are quite ready to assist, but must not be expected to take the lead. We watch the Christians ; many people join the Mohammadan religion, not because they believe it better than the Christian, but because they get some worldly benefit from it. The Mohammadans are always ready to help one another."

Mr. Booboo then said, "Although I am a Mohammadan there is no one in the country who would be more sorry than myself to see the church in which we are now sitting allowed to fall. I assisted under my late chief, Fa Dicki (Richard Wilkinson), in building it. All have received benefit from the Christian religion and feel an interest in the work, and if it were only a fowl that I had to give I would give it to aid in keeping the missionaries here."

After a time Mr. Charles Wilkinson rose and said, " I give my son Henry for the work of the Mission," placing him in the aisle.

Then after a pause Mr. Turpin, the chief missionary, said that two others had given themselves—William Harvey, a lad who had been with him for five years, and the young man Gomez, who had been acting temporarily as schoolmaster.

CHAPTER XIII.

Sad accident to mission boat—The Black Bagas—Tribal wars—Fire at Fotobah.

OST travellers' tales, and faithfully told stories of mission life, in wild and uncivilized countries, are generally, to a great extent, records of disasters, misfortunes, and constant disappointments. The story of the Rio Pongo is no exception. The list of boat accidents, with loss of life and property, is a peculiarly sad one. One of these was reported by Mr. Doughlin on July 22nd, in this year (1875). He had despatched the mission boat on Friday, the 16th, to Freetown, after taking the precaution to satisfy himself that the wind outside the river was favourable for its passage. Half an hour after midnight, just as she opened the bar, one of those sudden squalls, which are so frequent in July, came down the river and capsized her. There was a very strong ebb tide running, so that one man and six children were carried away at once. There were nineteen persons on board, all told—eleven men, one woman, and seven children. The remaining twelve clung to the boat and pieces of wreckage; but the woman becoming numbed, was soon washed away as her children had been. Mr. Thompson, the schoolmaster, was the first to reach the shore of one of the Mangrove Islands— but not before five in the morning—seven men were picked up by a canoe coming up the river, and the captain, the mate, and one of the passengers managed to swim to an island, and reached one of the Baga towns. The report of this reached Domingia on Sunday, and caused the greatest possible sorrow amongst the heathen and Mohammadans, as well as Christians. Besides the sad loss of life, the loss of the mission boat just at the time when the rains were at their height, was very serious, as so many people depended upon the station for supplies of food.

In September, 1875, Mr. Doughlin paid a visit to Mr. Turpin at the Rio Nunez, and on his return, while passing Long Island, at the mouth of the river, came across a race known as the Black Bagas, one of the most degenerate on the coast. Six men came alongside his boat begging for tobacco. Some was given to them, and, as they were going away (Mr. Doughlin says) "my eyes lighted on an idol in the bow of the canoe. I asked to be allowed to have a closer view of it, but was told it was their *quië* (greegree) ; another said 'it is their *berri*' (spirit) ; while one of the Bagas themselves called out, '*alla na'na*,' (it is God). It was some time before any of them would venture to touch it ; at last one of them

held it up, saying that it belonged to a friend, but
that if I would go to their town he would sell me
one. It was of wood, and made in the shape of a
man. I could not bear to hear the Susu boatmen,
themselves lately heathen, laughing at the ignorance
of the Bagas; and told them that they onght to do
something to help their brethern. Their reply was
'Master, the Black Bagas are not men, they are
cows;' *Nei mu findima abada* (they will never turn).
A little further on, several canoes passed us, filled
with women going to their farms; the most miserable
wretched-looking creatures my imagination had ever
pictured. They were nearly naked, exceedingly poor
and haggard, and apparently scarcely able to support
the children which were on their backs, much less
less to paddle their canoes. Christianity has truly a
great work still to do upon the coast of *the dark
continent*."

Two small tribal wars caused much confusion and
inconvenience upon the river about the months of
August and September, 1876. The first between
a combination of the Susu, Fullah, and Landuma
tribes, and the Mixii Fori, or runaway slaves, who
had from time to time escaped from neighbouring
tribes, and formed themselves into an independent
community. They live between the Rivers Nunez
and Pongo, in which district is situated a large
indiarubber forest, often a bone of contention between
them and the Susus. The second quarrel was between
the Susus and the Bagas, about a few acres of land
in the Fotunta district, said to belong to the Susus,
but claimed by the Bagas. On this miserable question

the country was kept in excitement and suspense for months.

One of the main incidents that marked the year 1877 was the fire at Fotobah, which destroyed a good part of the town, as well as the old church. This was the cause of considerable loss and discouragement to Mr. Clarke, the missionary at that station. He was on the point of erecting a new church, and did not, therefore, so much regret the old building, which had done its work and was about to pass away, but much of the timber for the new fabric was also destroyed, as well as the furniture and service books. Later in the same year it was determined that the station on the Rio Nunez, where a church had been built in 1869, by Mr. Duport, destroyed by fire in 1870, rebuilt and reopened by the Bishop of Sierra Leone, in 1871, and where a school had been doing good work under Mrs. Duport, should be finally abandoned—a sad though necessary act, in consequence of the great falling off in the funds of the Mission. The church was pulled down, and the doors, windows, bell, pulpit, lectern, reading-desk, font, communion rails, with some benches and boards were transferred to the Isles de Los, and used in the new church at Fotobah.

CHAPTER XIV.

Episcopal visitation—Conference—Death of Mrs. Lighthurn.

N 1878 the Bishop of Sierra Leone paid a visit to the Isles de Los, and in his report stated that at Fotobah he found twenty-two children in the day-school and seventy-eight in the night-school. The work there, and at the other five chief stations (Cockles Town, Boom, Rogbana, Crawford Island, and Cassa), was being successfully carried on by the Rev. R. J. Clarke and his catechist, Mr. Thompson. On Fotobah 355 persons had been baptized since May 3rd, 1855. After administering the rite of Confirmation to twenty-five persons, and holding a celebration of the Holy Communion, the Bishop went on to Fallangia, where he presided over an important conference of clergy and laity on the 18th and 19th, composed of the ordained missionaries, the native chiefs, and about fifty other laymen. Many practical resolutions were carried at the several sessions for the self-support of the Church at the Rio Pongo. Amongst others were the following :

i. That a capitation assessment of one bushel of ground nuts should be levied annually on every Christian ten years old and upwards.

ii. That all the schoolmasters and catechists should be examined on each visit of the Bishop.

iii. That a catalogue of the Mission property in each station should be sent to the Bishop, and a copy kept in the records of the place, so that the Mission's property might be known from that of the missionaries.

iv. That a native carpenter be kept permanently, who should go from station to station repairing the boats, dwellings, etc.

After the Conference a confirmation was held at Fallangia, and then, satisfied with the good work being done by Mr. McEwen, the Bishop proceeded to Domingia and inspected the Rev. P. H Doughlin's district. From thence the Bishop, in company with all the missionaries, went on to Farringia, where he introduced as catechist, Mr. David Brown, late student of Fourah Bay College, and a Licentiate in Theology of Durham University. The clergy were hospitably entertained and welcomed by the lady chief, Mrs. Lightburn, Mr. Lightburn, Mr. Marsden, and others, The Bishop held a service, at which he baptized two adults, British subjects. He also preached to a very large gathering of people. At the end of the service the Bishop pronounced the blessing, placing both his

hands on the old lady's head. He was very much
struck with her devotion. She was old (upwards of
eighty), very infirm, and unwell ; but still she would
not be prevailed on not to kneel. She said : " I am
not able to remain sitting while you are kneeling in
prayer. I fear God. I am not his equal ; I fear
him." The old lady spoke a good deal of English
while in conversation with the Bishop.

From Farringia the Bishop went to Bashia, on the
Fattalah branch of the river, where the C. M. S. first
settled in 1804 ; and as he stood looking at the ruins
of the old buildings, the King of Bashia and Chief of
Canoffee came to him begging for a schoolmaster.
The town was then (in 1878), and is now, under
Mohammadan influence. Having visited Canoffee,
and Lisso on the opposite side of the river, he
returned to Domingia, where he held a confirmation
and inspected the schools. Retracing his way to the
Isles de Los, he held a Christmas Eve service at
Fotobah, and inspected Mr. Clarke's schools. Unable
to reach Sierra Leone by Christmas, the Bishop
spent that feast in the mission boat with four Susus,
and arrived at Freetown, December 26th, 1878. At
this time the Rev. J. W. Hayward resigned the office
of Secretary of the English Committee, and his place
was taken by the Rev. G. F. Barrow.

During his stay the Bishop visited old Mrs. Lightburn at Farringia, prayed for her, and blessed her.
It was the last time that he was to see her, for on
the night of April 14th, she passed away. The
news was not communicated until the next morning
when a large cannon was fired. This was no ordinary

news in the neighbourhood of the Rio Pongo. The
very gun which formerly kept guard over the many
poor souls which she held in her hands, now poured
forth the tidings far and near that her own soul had
gone forth into the hands of God. The infirmities of
age had pressed heavily upon her ever since her
baptism, and at last she died somewhat suddenly.
In former days the death and burial of Mrs. Lightburn would have been very different. The usual
saraxa or offering to the dead would have been made,
and heathen rites performed. But now we cannot
doubt but that the merciful Father accepted the
offering which she made *to Him*, even at the eleventh
hour, of herself, her soul, and body ; and our hope is
that our sister "rests in Him."

CHAPTER XV.

Sad death of a missionary—Importation of spirits—Losses of the mission—Ordination at Freetown of Bishop Crowther—Consecration of Bishop Ingham—Proposed boarding-school—Bramaia Station.

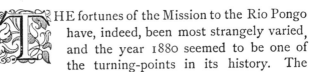 HE fortunes of the Mission to the Rio Pongo have, indeed, been most strangely varied, and the year 1880 seemed to be one of the turning-points in its history. The conversion of old Mrs. Lightburn to Christianity opened the door at Farringia, and now her death in the faith and fear of Christ Jesus firmly established the new station in that town. More workers were needed in order to keep the staff complete, and the Bishop of Sierra Leone, on Trinity Sunday, May 23rd, admitted Mr. Samuel Hughes, of Fourah Bay College, a Licentiate in Theology of Durham University, to deacon's orders to fill the vacancy at Fotobah. Mr. Hughes commenced his work on October 1st. By the time he was able to join his station his help had become a very sad necessity to the Mission, for in August the Rev. D Brown, who had begun at Farringia with so much

promise, was taken away. He had gone to Freetown, where he had been married on July 8th by the Bishop, to an old fellow-worker in the schools of that place. On August 11th he sailed in the cutter *Rotomba* for the Rio Pongo, taking with him all his wife's baggage and the furniture necessary to furnish a home for her, intending that she should follow by the next opportunity. The day after (the 12th), while passing the Bramaia bar, the vessel was capsized by a sudden squall, and nearly all on board were drowned, Mr. Brown among the number. The grief felt by the Farringia people was very great ; they sent special messengers at once down the river to see if the report which reached them were true. Mr. Doughlin, writing about his sad loss, said : "Poor fellow! he has gone from the work he loved so much, and the privations he bore so unmurmuringly, to receive the Master's approving smile in Paradise. I know something of work and its difficulty out here ; but the secret of his success was—he never returned from any work in church, school, or district without watering it with his prayers. He was at Farringia just a year and a couple of weeks, *and lived all the time in the house of a slave.* In this way he learned the language, the character, and the habits of the people, and was able to set them an example. Full of zeal, wisdom, and tact—full, too, of love, he could truly say : 'I have been going in and out amongst you.' I do not know what we shall do to fill his place." Again the work was left short-handed, and again the good Bishop came to the rescue by sending Mr. Samuel Cole in November to fill the post of catechist at Domingia, and thus set Mr. Doughlin more free to visit and encourage his fellow-workers.

An extract from Mr. Cole's first report gives some idea of the terrible evil by which England undoes so much of the good done by its missionaries. " A steamer came from England this day—a large vessel, filled completely with rum and gin.* There was not a single yard of cloth in her. When some one on board was asked if only spirits had been brought, he said : 'Yes ; and there is such a quantity of spirits on board that will make the whole Susu country drunk for weeks together.' Spirits demoralise the people and paralyse missionary efforts. The effects of spirits in the country are very painful."

The most striking events of the year 1881 were again of the nature of losses. Each of the three centres, Barbados, Africa, and England, lost its master from its head. The retirement of Dr. Mitchinson from the diocese of Barbados removed from the Board an able and willing friend. The resignation of Dr. Cheetham deprived the Rio Pongo of a father who had always taken the very greatest interest in the Mission, and been most self-denying in his efforts to advance the work—on one occasion spending Christmas Day at sea in a miserable boat rather than omit the visit to the stations which he thought it necessary to pay. Another and a severe loss was sustained by the death of the Rev. George Forster Barrow, the English Secretary, who died somewhat unexpectedly on November 17th, after

* Nine thousand casks of rum, 2600 demijohns of rum, 4000 cases of gin, and several thousand cases of assorted liquors.

three years of most indefatigable work in the interests of the Mission. His place as Hon. Secretary was taken by his brother, the present secretary.

The general work in the mission field progressed steadily, although neither Mr. Doughlin nor Mr. McEwen were in good health. The latter, being compelled to seek for rest and change of scene, visited England, where he did good work for the Mission by preaching and lecturing during the winter of 1881 and spring of 1882. He pressed much the long-felt necessity of opening a boarding-school, where some of the older boys might continue their education and be trained with a view to mission work, should they prove fitted for it.

On Christmas Day the new church at Farringia was used for service; but the formal dedication was put off until January 2, 1882, in order to give the other missionaries the opportunity of being present. Crowds of people attended the services, and eighteen adults were baptized. Mr. Doughlin preached the sermon from Gen. xxviii. 17. It was dedicated to St. Paul, as the lady workers of St. Paul's, Clifton, had done so much to help in its foundation. Mr. Morgan, the missionary, in his report, adds: " I was baptized at Paul's, Barbados, educated at St. Paul's school, and it would give me great happiness, if it should please God, that my ordination should take place at St. Paul's, Farringia, which I have striven to build ; " but this was not to be. Early in May, 1882, Mr. Doughlin, being in bad health, went to Freetown, and his place was supplied by Mr. W. C. Morgan, as catechist, a Licentiate in Theology of Durham University, and thus the Mission was left for the time with only two ordained clergy in residence, Mr. McEwen returning from England on June 9th.

On his settling down once more to work, Mr. McEwen's first care was to rebuild Mr. Clark's church at Fotobah, which had fallen into a very bad state of dilapidation. He proposed now to use stone for the walls and tiles for the roof, and the result was the erection of the first really permanent and strong church fabric in the Mission. The Christians of the island worked hard early and late, most unselfishly and without stint or grudging, feeling proud that they were permitted to take part in so good a work. This was the third church built or restored at Fotobah in eleven years.

In the beginning of the dry season Dr. Crowther, Bishop of the Niger territory, and an old Rio Pongo boy in the C.M.S. days, passed by Freetown on his way from England to his diocese. At the request of the English Committee he consented to hold an ordination at Freetown for the Mission during his stay there, as the See of Sierra Leone was still vacant. Accordingly Messrs. R. B. Morgan from Farringia and W. C. Morgan from Domingia were admitted to deacon's orders by Bishop Crowther on November 12th.

On February 24th Dr. E. G. Ingham was consecrated sixth Bishop of Sierra Leone, and directly afterwards sailed for his diocese.

The reports and letters of the missionaries having for some time strongly urged the necessity of establishing a boarding-school, into which the more promising children might be gathered from the day schools, the matter was taken up by the committee. The S.P.C.K.* promised a conditional grant of £125 towards the building fund, and by the help of the great efforts made by the secretary of the Clifton Association, the sum of £500 required for the buildings was soon collected. The erection of the buildings, however, were still delayed, pending the decision which was to be arrived at with regard to a matter of the greatest moment to the welfare of the Mission— viz. the appointment of a bishop, or European head to the work. It was felt that the school or college should be where the bishop was, and the most suitable place for the bishop's residence, or that of any European principal, seemed to be the Isles de Los. On the other hand, the Isles de Los being British territory, are included in the diocese of Sierra Leone, and thus the missionary-bishop would not be resident in his own diocese. The situation of the school was thus a difficulty until the question of a bishop had been decided. Ever since the beginning of 1884 the extreme need both of a bishop and a training college has been kept prominently in the foreground by the English committee, and a conditional promise of a grant of £2000 was obtained from the Colonial Bishopric's Fund, towards the endowment of a new see.

Early this year Chief Lewis Wilkinson, the son of the old Chief Richard Wilkinson, was taken ill, and on February 1st he died. It was he who as a young

* The Society has been a neverfailing helper of the Mission. It has made many grants to Churches and Mission Houses, and has printed the Susu Books which have been widely used.

man, nearly thirty years before, was sent by his father to convey Mr. Leacock from Tintima to Fallangia, on his first arrival at the Rio Pongo.

In 1885 a very strong appeal reached the committee from Bramaia, praying that a mission station might be opened in that place. It will be remembered that ever since the days of Mr. Neville, the same appeal had come from time to time. Now, mainly through the efforts of the Clifton Association and its indefatigable secretary, subscriptions were obtained to guarantee the salary of a catechist, and it was determined to undertake this new field of work. It was finally arranged that Mr. Miller should be sent there from Farringia. On Ascension Day, May 14, 1885, the Rev. R. B. Morgan was admitted to priest's orders by the Bishop of Sierra Leone, and thus there were two priests and two deacons on the staff.

CHAPTER XVI.

Statistics—Retirement of Rev. P. H. Doughlin—Death of Rev. J. W. Hayward—Archdeacon Holme's tour of inspection—Retirement of Barbados Board from main responsibility of Mission—Death of Rev. John Rigaud.

T the end of 1885 the French census reported that the population of the Rio Pongo proper (which comes of course under the influence of the Mission) is 36,544.[*] At Domingia, which is perhaps the most important centre, there were 533 entries in the baptismal register, and of this number 447 were still attached to the Church. At the town of

---

[*] " The Koba Bagas, the Kakisa Bagas, the Kullisokh-o Susus, the Kunde Virri Susus, the Black or Naked Bagas, the Mixii or Mikh-ii Fori or Black people (runaway slaves who have escaped from the neighbouring tribes), the Nallohs, and the Laudumahs. If to these are added the Bramaia Susus (a very considerable number) and the Kálum Bagas, opposite the Isles de Los, there are, counting the Bramaia and Rio Pongo Susus as one, ten distinct tribes and nations. Nine of them are bilingual, speaking their own languages and Susu as well."—*Rev. P. H. Doughlin's Report.*

Domingia itself there were 196, the rest being scattered throughout the district. The population of the several islands of the Isles de Los group was found to be 1200, of which number 713 persons were attending the ministrations of the Church. The baptismal register contained 525 names ; of these about 150 were people living at Conakry, on the island of Tumbo, which almost adjoins the mainland opposite to Factory IslanJ. At Farringia Mr. Lightburn estimated the population at 2000 ; at Bangalong and Sangha close by, 200 and 1500 respectively ; while the baptized Christians were at Farringia 200, and at Bangalong 27. Whilst on the subject of statistics, it is worth mentioning that on Sunday, June 28, 1885, the marriage of William da Silva and Hannah his wife, was celebrated in Fallangia Church. Da Silva was redeemed many years ago by some ladies at Clifton, and his wife and child in 1881 by another Clifton lady, but for some time after their redemption the /woman was unwilling to be married in church. Mr. Hughes, reporting this marriage, says, "when it is known that our native Christians are very averse to Christian marriage on account of the obligations imposed ; when it is also known *that we cannot boast of a dozen native marriages solemnized in the church since the commencement of the Mission,* all will agree that it is a matter of thanksgiving to Almighty God."

On July 8, 1886, the Mission suffered a great loss in the retirement of the Rev. P. H. Doughlin. He had done good work since he landed in Africa nearly nineteen years before, in October, 1867. After spending a short time. in England, Mr. Doughlin was appointed minister of St. Clements in South Naparima, Trininad, where he settled.*

A very old friend of the Mission was removed by death on August 2, 1886—viz. the Rev. J. W. Hayward, rector of Flintham, and commissary to Bishop Rawle of Trinidad. For many years, as its secretary, he was the mainspring of the undertaking. During this year Archdeacon Holme, of St. Kitts, who was in England on leave of absence, offered to visit the Mission and inspect and report on its state and present requirements. His offer was gladly accepted, and on December 19th he landed at Bullabina, opposite to the Isles de Los. After visiting Fotobah, he proceeded in an open boat to the Rio Pongo, inspected the stations of Domingia, Farringia, and Fallangia, to the great delight and encouragement of the missionaries. He brought home a full and valuable report on each station, its church, school, and buildings — besides photographs of places and people. From Fallangia, Archdeacon Holme † walked overland, accompanied by the missionaries, to Bramaia, where he had an interview with the king, and obtained from him a concession of land for a mission station and many promises of help. After leaving Bramaia the archdeacon sailed down the river to Dubrika, and thence to the Isles de Los.

The widespread poverty and distress which had fallen on the West Indian colonies during the last

---

* Mr. Doughlin revised, and was mainly instrumental in completing, the New Testament, the Order for Morning and Evening Prayer, and the Occasional Services in Susu. He also prepared a reading-book for schools in the same language, which has been published by the S.P.C.K.

† Afterwards Bishop of Honduras.

three years, from the sudden and serious depreciation of their staple products, rendered it no longer possible for the Barbados Board to raise the sum necessary to meet its engagements with the missionaries ; and in August letters were received from the president and the secretary, communicating, at the unanimous request of its members, this deplorable fact, and announcing the necessity forced on them to retire, at the close of the year, from the main responsibility for the support of the Mission, and from the future direction and control of its affairs. These they entreated the English committee to assume, promising to leave no effort untried to assist the committee under its onerous charge.

The alternative to this transfer, suggested by the board, was that an appeal be made to the venerable Society for the Propagation of the Gospel, to which the Mission has from the first been affiliated, to take it up henceforth as a part of its general work ; or, if the funds of that Society should be unequal to this additional charge, that a similar earnest request be made to the Church Missionary Society, already largely engaged in mission work on the West Coast, with a bishop at Sierra Leone within a day's sail of the Pongas country.

After communicating with all the bishops of the West India province, and after much anxious consultation, the committee decided that it was their duty to make the effort *to continue the Mission on its present distinct lines.* To this conclusion they were led by three main considerations : first, that they would not be justified in imposing on either of the

two great missionary societies this new burden,
supposing that either of them should be willing to,
accept it, unless it were the only means of saving
from extinction a work so manifestly blessed of
God ; secondly, that it has been felt by very many,
as well in the West Indies, as in the church at home
that it would be a reproach to those keenly interested
in the African race, if this cherished undertaking
were to be deprived of its distinctive character, and
the channel into which their alms and their sympathies
have been hitherto directed were to be dried up ; and
thirdly, that the encouraging report on the Mission
presented by Archdeacon Holme of St. Kitts, and
now in the hands of most of its friends, appeared to
the committee a manifest call upon them not to
shrink from assuming the responsibility delegated
to them by the Barbados Board.

At the end of 1887 the Bishop of Antigua, who had
for some time filled the office of chairman of the
English Committee, resigned the post, much to the
regret of all the members ; and the Rev. John Rigaud,
one of the earliest friends and supporters of the
Mission, was appointed.

On February 22, 1888, the church at Farringia, which
was a native building with a grass roof, was burned
to the ground. Some grass-fields adjoining had been
set on fire, and a strong wind which was blowing at
the time carried some of the burning grass on to the
roof of the church. Mr. Lightburn, the chief of
Farringia, at once set his people to work to rebuild
the walls, and it was proposed that the roof should now
be covered with tiles.*

* The tiles were given by the Sisters of the Church, Kilburn.

This year the English Committee lost its esteemed chairman, the Rev. John Rigaud, who passed away after a painful illness of some months. He had served on the committee for nearly twenty-five years. His place as chairman was taken by the Rev. H. W. Burrows, Canon of Rochester.

Christmas, 1888, saw the close of the thirty-fourth year, since the West Indian Church commenced its good work in Africa. Many and sore had the difficulties and trials of the Mission been, but throughout, God had been with his servants, and blessed their efforts. Never has more been done, and, humanly speaking, greater good resulted within so limited a field, than has been accomplished under God by the small band of faithful native clergy, catechists, and schoolmasters upon the banks of the Rio Pongo.

CHAPTER XVII.

HE year 1889 was marked by the death of Bishop Rawle, which took place on May 10th, at Codrington College, whither afte resigning the See of Trinidad, he had returned, to his old home in Barbados, there to consecrate the last days of his life, in his old college, to the duties of the Professorship of Theology. He had, however, overrated his strength, and within a few months of his entering upon the work, this devoted servant of Christ was taken to his rest.

The long cherished scheme of a boarding-school was now pushed forward to a practical issue in the Island of Cassa (Isles de Los); a suitable site was obtained and made over to the Mission by the Government. Before the building was commenced, the post of headmaster was offered to and accepted by Mr. C. W. Farquhar, master of the Mico Model

School at St. John's, Antigua, where he had already
had fifteen years of scholastic experience, and where
his work was highly appreciated.   After being
ordained deacon by Bishop Branch, he sailed with
wife and family to England on his way to the Isles
de Los, which he reached in October, 1890, and
where he immediately threw himself activity into the
work of preparation and organization.

The committee at home had now much to engage
their anxious deliberations, and were glad to welcome
the Earl of Stamford as a colleague.

CHAPTER XVIII.

Bishop Ingham's inspection—Death of Rev. Canon Burrows—Appoint-
ment of the Earl of Stamford as chairman of English Committee—
Supervision of Mission undertaken by Bishop of Sierra Leone—
The heathenish secret society.

N 1891 the Bishop made a thorough
inspection of all the stations. There
were services, confirmations, school ex-
aminations, and a conference of workers.
A serious blow was now aimed at the Mission
by the French authorities, who ordered all schools
to be closed where French was not taught; and
although every effort was made by the missionaries
to secure teachers, the difficulties proved to be
insurmountable, and the schools were accordingly
closed. Meanwhile the new school in British territory
was rapidly being completed, and Mr. Farquhar had
already gathered a goodly number of pupils around
him.

On the English Committee, too, an unexpected blow

fell by the death of the Rev. Canon Burrows, who had been its chairman since Mr. Rigaud's death in 1888. Lord Stamford now accepted the vacant chairmanship, an appointment received with general satisfaction, not only on account of his great interest in foreign missions generally, but also because of his experience and ability, his knowledge of the West Indies, and his special interest in the Pongas Mission.

Several new departures were now taken, and it may be said that from this time, the management of the Mission entered on a new phase entirely. The funds of the Mission were perceptibly dwindling, and the strictest economy had to be enforced. It had now become evident, too, that there was no longer any reasonable hope of securing the appointment of a bishop for the Rio Pongo, and the idea was finally abandoned. The venerable Bishop of Antigua proposed accordingly that the Bishop of Sierra Leone be invited to assume the charge of the Mission for so long a time as the arrangement should continue to be satisfactory both to himself and the committee. The proposals and rules submitted by the Bishop of Antigua were cordially agreed to, and the S.P.G., which partly supports the Mission, warmly approved of the scheme, as bringing the Mission more into apostolic order. More frequent committee meetings were now held and, the committee was fortunate enough to secure the active services of Dr. R. N. Cust, as one of its members. The missionaries, at this time, wrote repeatedly of the increase of Mohammadanism in the Rio Pongo, the baneful influence of polygamy, and the lapse of several converts, who were led astray on the re-appearance of " Simoi," the old heathenish secret society, abolished long ago in the Fallangia district by the late Richard Wilkinson.

CHAPTER XIX.

Opening of boarding-school—Plague of locusts—New church at
Fallangia—The thirty-eighth anniversary of the commencement of
Mission—Conference in London—Management and organization
—New station at Kambia—Mr. Cole's interview with "Bey Firma."

HE boarding-school was formally opened
on July 1, 1892, and on December 18th
Mr. Farquhar held his first examination
of pupils, the results of which were most
encouraging. The principal of Fourah Bay College,
and the Rev. Canon Taylor Smith also examined
the school, and sent letters expressing their satisfaction at the progress made in that short time.
Some anxiety was caused in 1893 by the repeated
visits of locusts. "These destructive creatures,"
wrote Mr. Cole, "made their appearance on January
28th, and took two hours and twenty minutes in
passing over. It looked very much as if there was
an eclipse during their transit. Their second visit
was made in April, when they continued till June,
devouring almost the entire rice-crop that was just

springing up. There was much unrest and con-
sternation among the people. Immediately after
the heavy rains their third visit was made, when
large quantities of guinea-corn, rice, and other plants
were devoured. The anxiety for the future is very
great, and already food is beginning to be scarce."
The new stone church at Fallangia, commenced in
1890, was completed by the end of May, and great
was the joy in and around that station when the
church was opened on June 4th. The congregation
was large, the service was impressive. Mohammadans
in large numbers came to witness the scene, and were
greatly pleased to see the church completed. They
were much interested when thirteen converts were
admitted by Holy Baptism into the Church, and the
Holy Communion administered to thirty recipients.

November 15th marked the thirty-eighth anniversary
of the arrival of the first missionaries, Leacock and
Duport ; and, in order to commemorate the day, a
special service was held in Fallangia Church, to which
crowds of worshippers were drawn. An interesting
meeting followed, when speeches were made expressing a desire for a Susu ministry. Testimony was
also borne by Mohammadans to the great value of
the Mission. One Mohammadan priest, indeed, openly
professed his love for the Church and interest in its
affairs. In October, 1894, an important and interesting Conference took place at the S.P.G. House in
London. The two chief representatives of the Mission
were present, viz. the Bishop of Jamaica, primate of
the West Indian Church, and the Bishop of Sierra
Leone, the head of the Mission in West Africa. The

Bishop of Jamaica raised the whole question of the
management and organization of the Mission, and
strongly advised the drawing up of more definite
instructions and regulations for the information of
persons, both clerical and lay, wishing to offer themselves for work. Another important matter was a dis-
cussion respecting the decision recently come to by
which it was determined to enter on a new field of work
at Kambia on the great Scarcies River. Owing to the
many difficulties put in the way of the missionaries
by the French authorities, it was felt that there
could be no longer much progress in the old stations ;
and the proposal to push forward further inland, and
open "fresh ground" in British territory, met with
hearty approval, both in the West Indies and at
home. The Bishop of Sierra Leone had recently
made a tour of inspection, and pronounced Kambia
to be in every way a most suitable locality for the
new enterprise. The inauguration of the work was
assigned to the Rev. S. Cole, in whom the committee
had every confidence ; indeed, the reception offered
him in this entirely heathen district was an earnest
of future success, and, with the blessing of God, it
held out hopes of great things to come.

Mr. Cole thus describes his interview with the Bey
Firma (King). As soon as he saw me, said : "Well,
has our friend last year come again (remembering
Mr. McEwen's visit last year). These people truly
keep their words ; they promised to come this year,
and they have come." After mutual salutation he
went in, changed his clothes, washed his feet, and
came to the place of hearing (this is a large piazza in

front of his house, where court is daily kept). Many people were present, say about thirty in all; and having taken his seat, he asked, "What is the news?" The Alikarli (Governor) then related to the whole assembly the Bishop's visit last year, and subsequently that of Mr. McEwen's, and that their object is to plant the Gospel of Christ in our country. How the Bishop has sent this missionary to commence the work, and that he promised to visit us some time afterwards. So saying, he presented the Bishop's letter to Bey Ferma, who handed it over to the next man, and on to the other till it was put in Mr. Johnson's * hand, who was asked to read it. The letter was read and explained in the Pimnee language, and the meaning was passed over to Bey Ferma, as is customary among them. This being done, Bey Ferma said, "I have heard." The Alikali then turned to Mr. Johnson and asked for the *word*. Mr. Johnson had forgotten about a present, and then said: "I don't understand you." "How did Mr. Cole come?" asked the Alikali. "How did the Bishop send him?" I then handed Mr. Johnson the cash, which I had brought with me for this purpose, and he passed it over to the Alikali, who in turn gave it to Bey Ferma. When he had received it, he said: "The news that Mr. Cole brings is a good one. Neither my father nor my grandfather knew anything of this. I am very glad of it. The missionary can stay in the country and do his teaching work. To show that I approve of it, I am the first to give him my son. This is from God, and we ought to hold it.

* A resident.

It is a good thing to have a school in our country so that our children can be taught." The other people spoke to the same effect, and five of them also offered their children to me for Christian instruction. After this I addressed them in the Susu language. The Pimnee language is widely spoken in Bey Ferma's quarter, while at Kambia the Susu language more ; but all understand Susu. They then brought us some food, which the Bey Ferma had ordered, as soon as he came, to be prepared for us. Before we left he also gave orders to the Alikali, in the presence of all the elders, and said : " Take the missionary back to Kambia, keep him there, find a good place for him where he can do his work freely. Tell him that I alone will not be able to keep him in the country, nor do all for him. I will send to tell the other kings around that there is a school at Kambia, and that they should send their children there for education. Give to the missionary any piece of ground he may require, and see that no one disturb him. When I go down to Kambia, I shall call to see him." With these words I left Bey Ferma's quarters, and returned to Kambia, humbly lifting up my heart in thankfulness to God for having prospered my undertaking."

CHAPTER XX.

N the early part of 1895 the Bishop of
Jamaica, in his address to his Provincial
Synod, reviewed the work of the Mission,
and sketched out its present circumstances
and future prospects, alluding in detail to the dis-
cussions which had taken place at the late Conference
he attended in London. He then alluded to a
proposed visit of the Bishop of Sierra Leone to the
West Indies in the following weighty words :—

" In connection with this subject I am justified in
mentioning to you, what has to some extent come to
your knowledge already, that the Bishop of Sierra
Leone has, partly through his connection with the
Rio Pongo Mission and in other ways, been led to
the conclusion that an effort ought to be made to
ascertain how far the West Indian Church can supply
men needed for the missions of the Church in Western

Africa generally. If it is in the order of God's Providence that this should come about, I believe the call will evoke the necessary enthusiasm, and the necessary devotion. I am rather inclined to think that the West Indian Church generally is suffering for want of some demand of this kind on its self-sacrifice. I do not underrate the value of lives of quiet, self-sacrificing devotion, which are being lived in our own times and under our own observation, and which compare not unfavourably with what is shown in the history of the Church even in bygone days of great effort and success. But I am thinking of heroic demands for complete and absolute self-surrender, for a zeal that places the whole life and the whole career on the altar of God, and that leads men to go forth as pioneers of Christianity and civilization into the cheerless and dark places of the earth, counting not their lives dear unto them."

The Bishop of Sierra Leone arrived in Barbados in the following June, and made his promised visit of inquiry. From Barbados he went on to the Leeward Islands and thence to Jamaica, returning home, *viâ* Bermuda and New York. Bishops, clergy, and laity alike gave him a hearty welcome, and co-operated most cordially with him in the objects he had in view.

A most interesting account of his tour was published by the Bishop as soon as he returned to England, under the title of " The African in the West Indies." *
Shortly after this, the primate of the West Indian Church issued a "Memorandum" respecting the

---

* London : Sierra Leone Diocesan Fund, 115, Chancery Lane, W.C.

Mission, in which he dealt with its constitution and organization. This memorandum was carefully considered by the committee at home ; also by the board in Barbados, and by the Bishop and missionaries in Conference in the Rio Pongo, and continued to engage their deliberations during the year.

Mainly through the untiring efforts of Miss Cole, secretary of the Clifton branch, whose zeal and self-denying labours in behalf of this Mission must here be recorded with the deepest thankfulness, a girls' boarding-school was now opened at the Isles de Los. Such an institution was the natural sequel to the similar one for boys, which proved so successful an undertaking.

The Rev. C. Farquhar says, on November 11th :—

"Your latest heart's wish was attained on 6th inst., when the girls' boarding-school was formally and solemnly opened. There was Choral Litany at the school chapel, Cassa, and a special office at the school house itself, and Miss Alice McEwen and Mrs. Duport are fully installed. The number at starting was small, but we do not despise the day of small things, and we have to face the fact that our people will find it harder to give up their girls for Christian training than the boys, but the cause being God's we cannot doubt that He will remove all our difficulties in His own good time. Mr. McEwen has made the place look well and cheerful."

An irreparable loss soon fell upon the English Committee, and indeed upon the whole Mission, before the year was closed. The venerable Bishop of Antigua, Dr. William Walrond Jackson, one of the original promoters of the Mission, and from its commencement its most loyal and loving supporter, was called to his rest. At the same time, the fact that he was spared so long and took such an unfailing interest in all that concerned the Mission up to the last, called forth the gratitude of all who had the privilege of being associated with him. The Bishop was born on January 9, 1811, and died November 25, 1895.

CHAPTER XXI.

New missionaries—Issue of regulations by English Committee—
Resignation of Dr. Ingham, Bishop of Sierra Leone—The year 1897
—Conference at Lambeth Palace—Fresh disasters—The hurricane of
1898—Death of Bishop Bree—Still signs of vigour in the Mission—
Abandonment of old mainland stations.

HE reader is now familiar with the un-
certainties and vicissitudes of this little
Mission, its encouragements and discouragements, its "ups and downs," its
story of life and death. It remains briefly to
record the events of the last few years, and so
bring the story down to the present time. In 1896
the Mission staff was once more recruited by the
addition of two new missionaries sent out by the
Church in Jamaica, Mr. W. F. Burris and Mr. F.
March, both being students of Codrington College.
A strong link is thus created between the Church in
Jamaica and the Mission in Africa, which is a matter
for thankfulness and gratification. In the month of
August the English Committee issued its final regulations for the future management of the Mission

founded mainly on the Bishop of Jamaica's memorandum. They were adopted after full consideration
and in consultation with the authorities in England,
the West Indies, and West Africa.*

Since the year 1883 the committee had found a
never-failing friend and counsellor in Bishop Ingham ;
but now, after more than thirteen years of faithful
labour, his episcopate, which had lasted longer than any
of his five predecessors, came somewhat unexpectedly
to a close : for he resigned the See of Sierra Leone
towards the close of the year. He had been wonderfully successful in originating and carrying through
a large number of useful schemes for the welfare both
of Church and colony ; and throughout his enormous
diocese, in Lagos and the Yoruba district, in the
colonies of the Gold Coast and of the Gambia, and
in the Canary Islands, the news of his impending
resignation was received with universal regret, and,
not the least, in the Rio Pongo Mission, where his
wise council and sound judgment will long be missed.
In his successor, however, the Rev. Canon J. Taylor
Smith, who was consecrated on May 27th (Ascension
day), 1897, the mission has already secured a warm
supporter—the new bishop being an old friend, and
one who is well acquainted with the Rio Pongo
Mission.

In the following July, in the great Jubilee year,
advantage was once more taken of the presence of
the West Indian bishops, who were in England and for
the Lambeth Conference, and who met the friends
of the Mission in the library at Lambeth Palace.

* See Appendix.

The primate of the West Indian Church, who had just assumed the title of Archbishop, sketched the efforts which had been made in each diocese of his province in behalf of the Mission, and acknowledged the obligations under which the West Indian Church lay, to the English Committee for its continued endeavours to second those efforts. "When times were fairly prosperous," said the Archbisbop, the church in the West Indies had sent its mission to the heathen, but the present financial conditions of the islands was now too notorious to need description. Their own churches were unprovided for, their own clergy, in many cases, unpaid, and whilst they would still do all in their power, it was quite clear that the out look was gloomy in the extreme." The other bishops spoke to the same effect. The year 1898 brought fresh disasters. The Report issued by the West Indian Commission, if it did not pronounce the doom of the sugar industry, practically obliterated all hope of return to the prosperity of former days for many a year to come. Then came the news of the terrible hurricane which swept over the islands with an almost unprecedented fury; St. Vincent and Barbados being the chief sufferers. Writing to the Admiralty of the disaster as it affected St. Vincent, the commander of Her Majesty's ship *Intrepid*, says—

"It is impossible to overstate the damage done to every town and village in the island, and to crops and works. The whole island has the appearance of having been fired through; utter desolation prevails everywhere. Hardly a green spot is to be seen

where before all was verdant and beautiful to look
upon ; the towns and villages, as viewed from the sea,
have the appearance of having been bombarded ;
churches, houses, and public buildings are mostly
levelled to the ground, and those that are still stand-
ng will have to come down and be rebuilt.   The
inhabitants are in a state of destitution, with no roofs
over their heads, excepting the shelters that have
been hastily raised for their protection from the
weather, which are not by any means adequate to
the number of the population ; and had it not been
for the very prompt assistance of the Government,
and of the ships ordered to their relief, the inhabitants would for the most part have starved."

The island of Barbados, too, from whence the
Mission derives so large a proportion of its funds,
was devastated to an alarming extent, and the closing of Codrington College was said to be within a
measurable distance—a calamity which the generosity
of English friends alone averted.   In the early part
of 1899 Dr. Herbert Bree, who had been Bishop of
Barbados since 1882, and president of the West
Indian Board, passed to his rest.   The funds avail-
able for the Mission from West Indian sources were
greatly diminished, and it appeared that a crisis had
indeed come, and that the days of the Mission were
numbered.   But who that has read these pages will
say that the work is not of God, or that an Unseen
Hand is not disposing all things according to His
godly wisdom?   As the present century draws to
its close, there are signs of fresh vigour and renewed
life in the Rio Pongo Mission.   The Bishop of Sierra

Leone has kindly found work in his diocese for Mr. Burris, who was ordained deacon on February 19th; and when the Rev. J. B. McEwen found that the Committee had to turn a deaf ear to his appeal for funds towards the new station at Conakry, he made a vigorous and praiseworthy attempt to raise the neccessary sum for a new church. The traders and settlers in this rapidly increasing centre readily responded, and his efforts were so far successful that the new church is already built, and was opened for Divine Service on January 4, 1900. A very serious decision has also been come to with regard to old mainland stations — Domingia, Farringia and Fallangia, It had long been foreseen that, owing to the exigences of the French occupation, the presence and work of the English missionaries would be, in the eyes of the French Government, unwelcome in those particular places.

In the providence of God it seemed to be clearly pointed out that the Mission of the West Indian Church has done its work in those places where it began nearly fifty years ago ; and if the scene of its labours is now, with reluctance, changed, yet it is, at the same time, made clear that fresh doors are being opened and new ground pointed out, where the light of the Gospel may be diffused, and souls brought to Christ. The Divine resources are inexhaustible, and God will not to be unmindful of His own.

APPENDIX I.

THE following is a list of the clergy who have worked during past years on the Rio Pongo :—

Rev. Jas. Hamble Leacock, S.C.C., 1855–56. *Died.*

Rev. J. H. A. Duport, S.C.C., 1855–73. *Died.*

Rev. Wm. Latimer Neville, M.A. Oxon, 1858–61. *Died.*

Rev. Abel Phillips, S.C.C., 1860–63.

Rev. Joseph Dean, 1860. *Died.*

Rev. J. A. Maurice, S.C.C., 1861–86.

Rev. J. F. Turpin, S.C.C., Cat. 1867, Deacon 1868, res. 1878.

Rev. P. H. Doughlin, S.C.C., Cat. 1867, Deacon 1871, res. 1886.

Rev. J. B. McEwen, S.C.C., 1871—

Rev. R. J. Clarke, S.C.C., 1874–80.

Rev. D. G. Williams, Fourah Bay, 1869, 70.

Rev. R. B. Morgan, Cat. 1875, Deacon 1882—

Rev. D. Brown, Cat. 1879, Deacon 1880, drowned 1880.

Rev. S. Hughes, L. Th. Durham, 1880—

Rev. S. Cole, Cat. 1880, Deacon 1888—

Rev. W. C. Morgan, 1882–84. *Died.*

Rev. C. W. Farquhar, Deacon 1890.

Rev. W. A. Burris, Deacon 1899.

Of this number four were Europeans, and twelve were natives. Three of the Europeans died, two at an advanced age, and the third of a chest complaint. Of the twelve native clergy, three have died—one after eighteen years' service—a second was drowned on the passage from Freetown, and the third died at Domingia after about two years' residence.

Rio Pongo Stations :
1. Fallangia opened, 1855 ; Rev. J. H. Leacock.
2. Domingia ,, 1861 ; Rev. A. Phillips.
3. Isles de Los ,, 1867 ; Rev. J. F. Turpin.
4. Rio Nunez ,, 1869; Rev. J. H. A. Duport.
   Closed, 1877
5. Farringia ,, 1879; Rev. D. Brown.
6. Bramaia ,, 1887 ; Mr. J. Miller.
7. Cassa ,, 1890 ; Rev. C. W. Farquhar.
8. Kambia ,, 1895 ; Rev. S. Cole.
9. Conakry ,, 1899; Rev. J. B. McEwen.

Rio Pongo Churches :
1. Fallangia (*St. James*).
   1st, 1865 ; burnt down, 1861.   Rev. J. H. Leacock.
   2nd, 1861 ; Rev. W. L. Neville.
2. Domingia. 1862; opened 1864. Rev. A. Phillips.
3. Rio Nunez (*St. Thomas*).
   1st, 1869 ; burnt, 1871.   } Rev. J. H. A.
   2nd, 1871 ; pulled down, 1877. } Duport.
4. Fotobah, Isles de Los.
   1st, 1878 ; Rev. R. J. Clarke.
   2nd, 1883 ; Rev. J. B. McEwen.
5. Farringia (*St. Paul's*).
   1st, 1881 ; Mr. Lightburn. Burnt January, 1888.
   2nd, 1888 ;   ,,
6. Bramaia, 1888 ; the King of Bramaia.
7. Conakry, 1899 ; Rev. J. B. McEwen.
8. Kambia, 1900.

APPENDIX II.

THE following regulations have been adopted after full consideration, and in consultation with the authorities in England, the West Indies, and West Africa :—

I. The control of the Rio Pongo Mission shall be in the hands of the English Committee in consultation with the Barbados Board (of which the Bishops of the West Indian Province are Vice-Presidents), and the Bishop of Sierra Leone.

II. The best preparation for candidates for work in the Mission is a thorough Schoolmaster's training, together with industrial training, whenever it can possibly be had.

III. It is not considered advisable that those going out to work in the Mission should be ordained in the West Indies ; nor must they expect to be ordained before they have thoroughly learnt an African language, in which there will be a Final Examination before Priests' Orders.

IV. It must be understood that the work which is being entered on is generally considered to be a life service ; at the same time, every application for furlough is considered on its merits.

V. Accepted candidates should, as a rule, proceed to

Africa unordained and unmarried. This would not, of course, apply to all cases ; such, for instance, as when men of some Diocesan standing offer themselves for work in the Mission. Three grades of salaries shall be recognized in the Mission : £120 for a Priest, £100 for a Deacon, and £50 for a Catechist. A Mission House is in all cases provided. Any addition of salary shall be on the recommendation of the African Committee.

VI. The present African Conference shall henceforth be recognized as the African Committee of the Mission, under the Presidency of the Bishop of Sierra Leone. The members of this Committee shall be—

(1) All the Clergy of the Mission.

(2) Any Catechists considered (through experience and capacity) specially worthy of appointment by the other members of the Committee.

(3) Such local laymen as may be nominated by the Bishop and approved by the other members of the Committee.

The Committee shall meet at least twice a year for the business of the Mission.

VII. It shall be understood that all communications to the English Committee as regards salaries, leave, ordination, and the like, shall come through this local administrative body. And it shall also be a standing order that an estimate for the ensuing year shall always be submitted by the African Committee at the end of each year.

VIII. Each West Indian Diocese shall henceforth train its own men, and endeavour to raise annually a sum equivalent to the annual cost of maintenance of those men ; and through its Auxiliary Association, remit, as heretofore, to the English Committee, from year to year, whatever amount it can give to the General Fund of the Mission, it being understood that the English Committee shall decide, in consultation with the Bishop of Sierra Leone and the local

Conference, whether a given vacancy can be filled up or a given new station occupied, and that all such nominations be subject to the final approval of the Bishop of Sierra Leone.

IX. It will be most desirable that the Auxiliary Association in each West Indian Diocese should diffuse information and correspond about the work from time to time.

X. It shall be an instruction to the African Committee to endeavour to arrange for an Annual Conference of as many of the Mission workers as possible, both for spiritual edification and for mutual conference on subjects connected with the Mission. The time and place would be entirely at the discretion of the African Committee.

XI. Candidates for work in the Mission should in all cases apply, in the first instance, to the Bishop of the Diocese in which they reside, and must also undergo a medical examination in the West Indies, and be certified fitted for the work.

XII. Missionaries are expected to proceed from the West Indies direct to Africa. It is not considered desirable that they proceed *viâ* England.

> Approved by the English ⎞
> Committee in presence of ⎟
> the Secretary of the Barba- ⎬ STAMFORD.
> dos Board and the Bishop of ⎟
> Sierra Leone. ⎠
>
> *August* 11, 1896.

THE END.